# God Gave His WORD

### An Enlightening Look
### Into Who Jesus Is

## WAYNE FROST

Paperback ISBN 978-1-960007-63-6
eBook ISBN 978-1-960007-64-3

Published by

**Orison Publishers, Inc.**

PO Box 188

Grantham, PA 17027

www.OrisonPublishers.com

To my wife Joy.
God has blessed me.

**In Obedience to His Will**

"No one is to appear before me empty-handed"
(Exod. 34:20c NIV).
I am no longer "empty-handed."

# Acknowledgments

T hank you, Keith Carroll, for your willingness to assist an unknown, aspiring writer with such gracious, knowledgeable
assistance and expertise. I appreciate your extraordinary encouragement, patience and presence during this endeavor. May you
always be blessed.

# Table of Contents

# Preface

This book is a powerful discussion about the Bible's narration of pre-creation, creation, the promised birth of Christ, God, His plan for us, and His presence in our lives. Holy Scripture is referenced throughout with explanations, comments, definitions and interpretations to hopefully give the reader additional insight. Many referenced scriptures have discussion in familiar context. The Bible contains beautiful and compelling passages. Nothing in this book replaces, contradicts or changes the Holy Scripture. God is forever and never changes. His WORD, Jesus Christ, came as the fulfillment of His plan and design for us from before the beginning.

# Introduction

I spent my life as an attorney and am now a sitting judge. Service to God is not limited to the ministry but takes many forms, and we should use whatever talents God has given us in His service according to His will. As a lawyer, I uniquely experienced an understanding of words and their meanings. This book shares insight, with prayers and passion, for your new understanding of Jesus.

This book is not an introduction to Jesus. In fact, I believe my readers already know about Jesus. My heartfelt prayer is that your spirit will be moved beyond knowing and into an understanding of Jesus as never before. Questions will be answered with the intention to expand that understanding.

Likely most who have read their Bibles will have never contemplated some of the truths this book unveils. It was only after several complete readings of the Bible in several translations that I understood what I now share with you. I believe your understanding of Jesus will be exponentially enhanced, uniquely blessing your spirit.

You will contemplate Jesus, but you will do so on a new and different level. The apostle Paul wrote to the Colossians, "My goal is that they may be encouraged in heart and united in love, so that they may have the full riches of complete understanding, in order that they may know the mystery of God, namely, Christ, in whom are hidden all the treasures of wisdom and knowledge" (Col. 2:2–3 NIV).

Paul distinguishes between knowledge and wisdom, as did King Solomon when, in prayer, he asked God for wisdom and knowledge to lead and govern his people (see 2 Chron. 1:10). The "mysteries" of God are far deeper than knowing that He is in heaven and that heaven is a real place.

During my formal education, a classmate had what is called a "photographic memory." After reading any page from any book, he could recite its contents verbatim. Despite his memorization of the material, he failed his first essay examination. He knew what the information said, but apparently he could not apply it.

King Solomon possessed both knowledge and wisdom as "measureless as the sand on the seashore" (1 Kings 4:29b NIV). In reading this book, you will experience more than just knowing about the depth of God's love; you will also more fully understand that love.

Imparting information is not the same as demonstrating it. Jesus told us and showed us His power over death. In considering Jesus' last words on the cross, "It is finished," He was not admitting defeat; rather, He was pronouncing completion of the plan for our salvation (see John 19:30 NIV). Remember, we had lost immortality when Adam and Eve sinned and were denied access to the Tree of Life.

A more complete understanding of why we can have immortality again, how it was given back to us, and who was the architect of this plan is detailed here in this book. When we understand something, we learn more. John, the disciple whom Jesus loved, knew what the other disciples knew, but we will come to realize just how much more he understood.

John's writing introduces us to the discernment of the "mysteries" Paul references in his letters (see 1 Cor. 4:1, for example). We will explore what John understood through a discernment of biblical truths that reveal those "mysteries." A comprehensive, freshly considered reception of familiar scripture reveals a profound reality.

Read to discern what few others do about Christ. Take time to dwell upon each chapter to focus anew on understanding the detailed scriptural information being analyzed. "The fear of the Lord is the beginning of knowledge" (Prov. 1:7a NIV). Join with me as we go beyond mere knowledge and venture into a greater understanding of Jesus.

Through discernment your faith will be strengthened and your questions answered. Glory to God and His WORD.

CHAPTER ONE

# The WORD Was First

Some of the most compelling and informative scriptures of the Bible appear in the Gospels of John and Luke. It is John the Baptist's "testimony" and Luke's "investigation" that reveal information that corroborates the scripture in Genesis.

As a lawyer and now a judge, *testimony* refers to a statement given under oath as truthful, reliable, and having evidentiary value. It is more than a mere statement, speculation, guess or suggestion. Trial witnesses are sworn to tell the truth, the whole truth and nothing but the truth.

Typically witnesses testify about things or events they observed or experienced, or they testify about matters determined through investigation or testing. They are usually called in order of significance. Eyewitness testimony is common, as is police personnel testimony about information obtained through their investigation. Event participants typically relate their involvement or actions.

It is unacceptable and improper for an ordinary lay witness to testify and give his or her opinion for the jury to consider as factual because only those recognized as "experts" by the court may give relevant opinion testimony, and they can do so only in their field of expertise.

Having appeared as counsel in several hundred jury trials, one of the most rewarding experiences I have enjoyed is observing a jury react to a particular witness's testimony concerning a vital part of a case. In one particular case alleging an assault in which the victim's ear was bitten off, the witness replied, in response to a question, that he had not actually seen the ear being bitten off but knew the defendant had done it because he saw the defendant spit the ear out of his mouth!

During a trial an individual will not be called to testify unless his or her testimony is relevant, or having material or evidentiary value. If someone knows nothing about the case, then calling that person to testify would be a total waste of time and seem foolish. Luke's investigation and John the Baptist's testimony contain vital, relevant and factual information about Christ.

In my early career as an investigator and later as a trial lawyer, I knew that before a witness "testifies" about a matter, it is imperative to learn the details of his or her anticipated courtroom testimony. A thorough investigation detailing scientific analysis, fingerprint comparisons, crime scene photographs and other elements are important. Luke obviously understood how important it was to relate factual details derived from his investigation.

## Luke's Investigation

Luke tells us in his narrative that he "carefully investigated everything from the beginning" and so can relate details with "certainty" (Luke 1:3–4 NIV). These detailed facts concern Jesus as well as John the Baptist's connection to divine prophecy. Luke's investigation, John the Baptist's testimony, and the angel Gabriel's messages to Mary and Zechariah, along with everything occurring as had been foretold, reveal an undeniable truth.

It was the angel Gabriel who came to Zechariah in the temple and informed him that he and his wife Elizabeth would be given a son, to be named "John" (see Luke 1:13,19). John would be filled with the Holy Spirit even from birth and would go before the Lord (see Luke 1:17). We learn that John was sent by God to be a "witness" to the light who was "in the world, and…the world was made through him" (John 1:8,10a NIV).

When Elizabeth was six months pregnant, the angel Gabriel appeared to the virgin Mary in Nazareth to inform her that she would become pregnant with a son, to be named Jesus. Gabriel also related that her relative, Elizabeth, was already six months pregnant (see Luke 1:26–37).

When I was a criminal investigator, any information corroborated from different sources was deemed especially credible. Crime scene fingerprints, video surveillance and eyewitnesses' identification are all corroborative and together establish the facts.

During one of my investigations, that of a particularly grisly murder, there were bloody shoe impressions at the scene. The perpetrator, who was located not far away, had the victim's blood on his shoes, and the soles of his shoes matched the shoe impressions from the scene. This fact, along with other incriminating evidence, left but one conclusion about who the murderer was.

Luke's investigation also leaves us with only one conclusion, which we discern as we continue reading about Mary's visit to Elizabeth in the hill country of Judea. As soon as Mary greeted Elizabeth, John "leaped" in the older woman's womb. Elizabeth then exclaimed, "Blessed are you among women, and blessed is the child you will bear" (Luke 1:41–42b NIV).

It is important to note here that Mary had not yet explained to Elizabeth that she was to become pregnant by the Holy Spirit. However, Elizabeth knew as soon as the baby inside her moved. Remember, at this time Elizabeth was already six months pregnant, and Mary stayed with her three more months (see Luke 1:56).

I believe it is a fair conclusion that Mary was there when John the Baptist was born. There is no other obvious explanation for Mary staying another three months but to be a help to Elizabeth and be there for John's birth. After John's birth, Zechariah declared that John would go "before the Lord to prepare the way for him" (Luke 1:76b NIV). Zechariah knew this directly from the angel Gabriel.

Obviously, John the Baptist was born before Jesus, since Elizabeth was already six months pregnant when Mary visited. Whether Mary was already pregnant at this time or just anticipating becoming so isn't completely clear, but, regardless, we know that she gave birth to Jesus not long after John was born.

In reviewing events, beginning with Elizabeth's becoming pregnant on through the birth of Christ, Luke gives important details using the information he obtained through investigation, details that are verified by timelines of history regarding the Roman rule. Caesar Augustus was the Roman ruler at the time of both births (see Luke 2:1). Some thirty years later, John the Baptist and Jesus both begin their ministries (see Luke 3:23).

At the "fifteenth year of the reign of Tiberius Caesar" is when the word of God came to John the Baptist in the desert (Luke 3:1–2 NIV). We also see him preaching that "all mankind shall see the salvation of God" (Luke 3:6 AMP). It was at this time that John the Baptist began baptizing and preaching repentance (see Luke 3:3,16).

## John the Baptist's Testimony

Because we know that both John the Baptist and Jesus began their earthly ministries in their thirties, it's obvious that their respective births were close in time. Despite the mortal birth order, John clearly describes Jesus as being first. In John 1:15 (NIV) he states: "This is the one I spoke about when I said, 'He who comes after me has surpassed me because he [Jesus] was before me.'" *Was* is used as a past tense verb delineating something that occurred previously in time.

Twice in John 1:15 John the Baptist refers to Jesus as "was" rather than predicting Jesus with such words as "to be" or "will be." The statements John makes are profound because he "testifies" to this information. He isn't giving it as his opinion but as actual fact. Obviously, John the Baptist had received a divine revelation from God concerning Jesus.

John the Baptist tells us that he is not worthy to untie the sandal straps of the "one who comes after me" (John 1:27b NIV). So, he is merely announcing Jesus' impending arrival. He is proclaiming what was revealed to him so that the people can prepare to receive Jesus.

In stating "one who comes after," it is clear that John the Baptist is letting everyone know that Jesus, who existed before our earth was formed, would be arriving. John, who was present in the moment, referred to Jesus as having existed before him, and he said they would soon experience Him. He was making "straight the way for the Lord" (John 1:23c NIV).

In television talk shows, the host is already before the audience for the purpose of introducing the next guest. The guest is backstage but has not yet made his or her entrance. John the Baptist knows Jesus is coming and is informing his "audience." His role was to introduce Jesus, who was coming to baptize with the Holy Spirit because John knew He was the WORD.

In reading through further passages in the Gospel of John, we see John the Baptist "testifying." "This was He of whom I said, 'He who comes after me is preferred before me, for He was before me" (John 1:15b NKJV). This "testimony" reveals that John is, without any doubt, referring to Christ and verifying His divine preexistence.

According to Genesis 1:1 (NIV), "In the *beginning* God created the heavens and the earth" (emphasis added). Most of us have read this passage likely without contemplating the meaning of "beginning." Since God has no beginning, the "beginning" mentioned in this scripture cannot be referring to the beginning of everything. God was, is and will forever be. He has no beginning and no ending. (See Revelation 1:8.)

It is clear from these combined passages that the "beginning" is referring only to the earth and the beginnings of life on earth, including the creation of the first man, Adam, and first woman, Eve. God was not referring to His beginning.

God tells us, literally, that He is "God Almighty" in Genesis 35:11 (NIV). "The number of his years is past finding out," says Job (36:26b NIV). According to accounts in Job, God asks, "Where were you when I laid the earth's foundation?" (Job 38:4a NIV). "Or who laid its cornerstone, when the morning stars sang together, and all the sons of God [angels] shouted for joy?" (Job 38:6b–7 NKJV). John the Baptist also clearly knew who laid the earth's foundation, and he tells us!

John 1:1 (NIV) states, "In the beginning was the Word, and the Word was with God, and the Word was God." This is the earth's beginning as denoted in Genesis 1:1. The spelling of "Word" is particularly important and revealing because here it is begun with a capital letter, obviously denoting a name.

John's testimony reveals that Jesus was that "Word," which "was" with God and "was" God. Even though John the Baptist was born prior to Jesus' becoming flesh through a virgin birth, his use of the past tense verb *was* indicates that, before becoming flesh, Jesus existed when the earth was formed. He was the WORD.

Jesus, being born as mortal flesh, was God giving His WORD, who "was with God" and "was God."

## CHAPTER TWO

# Prophecy Fulfilled

Matthew describes in his Gospel how the birth of Jesus came about. He doesn't use the word *testimony* or tell us how he arrived at his accounts of Jesus' divine birth. He does tell us that Jesus was conceived through the Holy Spirit (see Matt. 1:18). He also states that the babe was to be named Jesus "because he will save his people from their sins" (Matt. 1:21b NIV).

All was to occur in fulfillment of what was written in the Old Testament through the prophets. In fact, Matthew tells us that John the Baptist was preaching of Jesus as the one foretold by the prophet Isaiah.

### "The Christ Is Coming"

Isaiah tells us that, apart from the Lord, "there is no savior" (Isa. 43:11b NIV). He says that there is no god apart from the righteous God and savior; there is none but Him (see Isa. 45:22). We are further told by Isaiah that God is the first and the last, and that His "own hand laid the foundations of the earth" (Isa. 48:12–13a NIV).

Again, we have reference to the WORD. Isaiah states that the "word" of our Lord "endures forever" (Isa. 40:8b NIV). Isaiah makes plain that God is real, that it was He who created all things, making mention of the mountains, islands and animals; that He knows all the stars by name; and that He is the everlasting God (see Isa. 40:6–31). Probably the most powerful reference to God in this portion of scripture is this: "See, the Sovereign Lord comes with power, and he rules with a mighty arm. See, his reward is with him, and his recompense accompanies him" (Isa. 40:10 NIV).

I believe Isaiah foretells of Jesus in these passages and of John the Baptist's introducing Him. Isaiah references *savior, word, arm, reward* and *recompense*. In clarifying these descriptive terms, *savior* is defined as one who saves, Jesus Christ; *reward* means something given in return for something done; *recompense* can also mean reward or compensation; and *arm* is the upper limb of a human body and thus a part of someone, or, in military terms, a weapon.

So, "the Sovereign Lord" coming with rewards, compensation and with His arm to rule for Him informs us that God created all and is coming to reward those who apparently had done something worthy of reward, compensating them in some way, while ruling over mankind.

As an attorney, I often see rewards offered by Crime Stoppers and other entities for information assisting in solving a crime. Sometimes rewards are posted for lost pets or other information. Compensation is often the referenced reward.

In past times, I often heard a father referring to his son as his "good right arm"—the one who might take over the family business or take on some other great responsibility. Christ is the one who bears the responsibility of redeeming mankind.

These passages are quite prophetic, reassuring people that God will "come down" to "save" them (Isa. 31:4; 35:4 NIV). Isaiah reminds us that He does not take back His words (see Isa. 31:2). So when Isaiah tells us, "For to us a child is born, to us a son is given…and he will be called Wonderful Counselor, Mighty God, Everlasting Father, Prince of Peace," he is speaking of Christ's coming (Isa. 9:6 NIV).

What we don't hear from Isaiah is exactly how or when Christ will come; all we do know is that Jesus would be born of a virgin and from someone in King David's lineage (see Isa. 7:14; 11:1; Luke 1:32). Luke traces Jesus' lineage back through Joseph, who was also a descendant of King David (see Luke 3:23–31). God is telling mankind through Isaiah about His plans for salvation.

Since we know that God's word is absolute, we can know of things to come. I believe that God never told Isaiah a definite date for Jesus' birth for a number of reasons. Primarily, those ruling would likely try to take measures to prevent the prophecy from ever being fulfilled, however futile those measures would surely have been. Perhaps efforts would have been made to eliminate descendants of David; perhaps the government would have tried establishing someone else as a "fake" savior for the advantage of the ruling classes.

God, of course, knew when, how and where the birth would occur. With God mistakes are not made, and no human effort can thwart His plan. Even though Herod discovered Jesus' birth from the wise men and had every firstborn male of Bethlehem killed, God had planned ahead for Jesus' safety (see Matt. 2:16).

Herod surely must have heard of the prophecies of Jeremiah that Israel would be restored from King David's line (see Jer. 33:15). As with most tyrannical rulers, power is everything, so Herod was fearful and would have done anything to ensure his continued position.

Jeremiah informs us that God told him the "days are coming" when the "good promise" He made would be fulfilled (Jer. 33:14 NIV). The New English Translation (NET Bible) says it is a "gracious promise." *Gracious* is another word for kindness or compassion. *Compassion* means being sympathetic or having great sympathy. In other words, God saw, felt and understood the human condition.

Nothing is hidden from God and nothing is unknown to God. Further, He also knew there was nothing that we, as humans, could do to alleviate our present condition or our ultimate demise. God would have to intervene, for nothing else and no one else could. This is what God meant in saying He would come to "save" mankind and "come down" (Isa. 31:4; 35:4 NIV).

It is difficult to understand God's being born in human form while still remaining fully God. The Church explains this concept as God's being a Holy Trinity: Father, Son, and Holy Ghost; all in one and one in all. While this explanation does offer a concept as close to what we cannot fully grasp in human understanding that it can, we do know what God declares and faith supports.

We will explore this topic further in later chapters. For now, just realize that there are things we cannot understand even in our own three-dimensional world. God is not bound by the limitations of our three-dimensional world. He created this world in its three dimensions and all the things in it. If He were bound by the limitations of our three dimensions, then He would have limitations.

### Some Things We Just Won't Understand

Logically, we can understand that God is multidimensional, that He is not bound by human laws of physics, spatial limits, travel, boundaries, barriers, gravity, etc. He is without limit. We can think of fish living in a body of water, which is a two-dimensional realm. They do not live in our three-dimensional world and cannot comprehend it.

In this three-dimensional world, we observe some things existing within these dimensions that are unlimited, such as no two snowflakes being the same, no two zebras having exactly the same stripes, no two box turtles having identical shells markings, or no two Dalmatians with the same spot patterns. There are other examples in nature that we can observe yet not explain.

We know that water can freeze and become ice, then thaw and become water again. Imagine how a tribesman in the deepest tropical jungle might react at seeing ice for the first time, then marvel at watching it become water or seeing it apparently "disappear" when it evaporates into air.

When I was a child, I would catch caterpillars, put them in a jar, and give them grass, leaves and other plant matter to eat, then wonder and marvel at seeing them "disappear." Upon closer observation, they had not disappeared; they had merely changed into another state of being when they entered their pupa or chrysalis stage.

But, when they emerged from their chrysalis (cocoon) as butter-flies rather than still as caterpillars, it was quite miraculous! Diamonds were once lumps of coal. Tadpoles become frogs. Wood can become petrified, becoming stone. We find petrified dinosaur bones, proving they existed, but we have never seen a live one.

Humans can construct a good many things, and we can utilize the resources of our world to manage, sustain, improve or assist human life. We cannot "create," however. Some may argue this point, but it is clear that manipulating, arranging, building, constructing, assembling or utilizing is not creating.

We may lengthen life or preserve life, but we cannot create life. We cannot reanimate a corpse. We cannot create a butterfly; we can only watch its transformation from egg to caterpillar, to chrysalis (cocoon), then finally to its emergence as a butterfly.

This, I believe, is why sometimes God is referred to as "Creator." Farmers can plow, plant, fertilize and irrigate, but only God can make the seeds sprout. As this quote—often attributed to Robert Schuller— says, "Anyone can count the seeds in an apple, but only God can count the number of apples in a seed."1

There is no doubt that God can appear in any form He so desires. He can speak to us in any language; He can speak in ways other than language, including dreams; and He can relate to us in any way He chooses to affect our better understanding. Here, He used prophets to foretell His coming.

In those days there was no internet, television, radio or world news networks. Communication was written and spoken. I believe signs, wonders and miracles were used to gain as much attention and awareness as possible. Those events reinforced the information related by the prophets.

"Word of mouth" was perhaps the most effective means of communication at that time. Anyone who witnessed the miracles associated with prophecy would relay the information as verification of all that was foretold. Anyone who heard about a certain event to come, then actually saw it, would give credibility to the source of that information.

It is the same today. If the evening weather forecast indicates rain in the morning, and then we see rain falling when we awaken in the morning to get ready for work, we will ascribe a certain credibility to the meteorologist. God's credibility was exhibited throughout biblical text and through the prophets.

CHAPTER THREE

# God's Unlimited Power

In our previous chapter, we made mention of our three-dimensional world. As we consider the limitations of three dimensions, let us also understand that God is not bound by the limitations of our world. Logically, it is apparent that if God were constrained by three dimensions, then He could not have created our world.

There are numerous instances in the Bible of God's appearing in different forms, interacting with us (mankind) through different circumstances, and relating to us in various ways. We as humans are not able to manifest as a cloud, a burning bush, a pillar of fire or anything other than a human form. God came in every form, including the human form.

### He Cares

The WORD became flesh and dwelled among us (see John 1:14). And beyond fulfillment of prophecy, we must wonder, "Why?" I believe the simple answer is that God wanted face-to-face interaction with us. Jesus experienced every human condition that we might face. He already understood our every emotion, our every concern and our very human existence, but, in becoming flesh, He could show us He understands and cares.

Everyone learns in different ways. We can read information; we can hear information; we can experience information; we can feel information. If we are told how to perform a certain task, we may understand, but if we are shown and told, then the understanding exponentially increases.

As a practicing attorney for more than thirty years, I tried to remember the adage spoken by Teddy Roosevelt that "nobody cares how much you know, until they know how much you care."1 My clients often exclaimed how impressed they were with my legal abilities, but what they were more impressed with was how I actually cared about helping them.

During my law practice, I was often appointed in state and federal court to some of the most difficult criminal cases. Since most of those defendants were incarcerated while awaiting trial, jail conferences were necessary. One particular client, during my first three visits, seemed uninterested, inattentive and disrespectful. On my fourth visit to confer with him, his attitude had changed. He finally looked at me, commenting, "You really care, don't you?"

My regular, frequent attempts to interact with him convinced him that I was really trying to help him despite his lack of cooperation. He saw how much I cared, and he appreciated my interest. He knew he was in trouble, but he needed to know I cared far more than he needed to know anything else.

When we read the Book of Exodus, we understand that a human cannot look upon the face of God. Moses wanted to see God face to face, but God told him no human could do so and live (see Exod. 33:20). God first spoke to Moses as a burning bush (see Exod. 3:2). Then later He spoke to Moses as a dense cloud, but He did so within hearing of the Israelites so they could hear and always trust whatever was relayed to Moses (see Exod. 19:9).

As the Israelites wandered through the wilderness to the Promised Land, God went before them as a pillar of cloud during the day and a pillar of fire at night, and sometimes He appeared as a thick darkness. God would "come down" to the entrance of the tent of meeting in the form of a pillar of cloud. (See Exodus 13:21; 20:21; and 33:9.) God wrote on the tablets of stone with His finger (see Exod. 31:18).

God gave instructions to Noah for building the ark (see Gen. 6:14). Noah was told to "bring" into the ark two of all living creatures (Gen. 6:19a NIV). Notice that Noah was not told to "gather" those animals, but to "bring" them into the ark. God must have communicated with those animals so they would arrive at the ark for Noah to "bring" them inside.

A Cheyenne pastor I know had tried in vain for years to convert his father to Christianity. It troubled him greatly that his own father had not accepted Christ and still practiced the "old ways." One day he visited his father who lay dying in the hospital. Imagine his shock and surprise when his father told him that he believed now. His father explained how Jesus had appeared to him and spoken with him fluently…in the Cheyenne language!

God can and will communicate with us in any form, in any manner and in whatever way is the most effective. He wants interaction with us. We matter to Him. This is the reason He came to us. In coming to us, He could demonstrate how much He cares and the extent to which He will go for us.

### He Wants to Be With Us

Jesus, the WORD, was with God and was God (see John 1:1). In understanding the scriptures, consider the angel Gabriel's message to Mary. He told her that she had pleased God and then further stated, "You will conceive and give birth to a son, and you are to call him Jesus" (Luke 1:31 NIV). Then, in Luke 2:5 (NKJV), she is described as being "with child."

This is important because, in the Gospel of John, we read how "in the beginning was the *Word*, and the *Word* was with God, and the *Word* was God" (John 1:1 NIV, emphasis added). Mary was "with" child and the WORD was "with" God. The significance in each instance is that "with" means to be a part of; a pregnant woman's child is part of her body, and Jesus was both part of God and was God.

Jesus, God's WORD, came in earthly form according to prophecy. He wanted us to see Him face to face, which we would not have been able to do and live while He was in His heavenly form, according to God's conversation with Moses (see Exod. 33:20). But, in earthly form as a human man, we could interact with Him and look upon Him without harm.

We see how God interacts, communicates and demonstrates, while also experiencing in human life form the same challenges and feelings—every emotion—exactly as we (His creation) do. This chapter is important because it demonstrates why God took human form. "For with God nothing will be impossible" (Luke 1:37 NKJV).

In reading scripture, we read *who* the WORD was; *what* the WORD did; *when* all came to pass, according to prophecy; and *where*, historically, events transpired. Now we can understand at least part of the *why*. When I was a law enforcement officer writing my reports, my formula for a good, complete report was answering "who, what, when, where, and *why*."

In the Book of Exodus, God told Moses that He would come to him in a cloud and speak to him so the Israelites could also hear and always trust Moses (see Exod. 19:9). Someone else telling us what another said is quite different from our hearing it for ourselves. God knew this because He created us. He also never wanted what Moses said to be doubted.

There have been times when I have listened to exasperated people commenting about how they don't think God understands. Nothing is further from the truth! The WORD came in human form, through human birth; grew and matured as a human; then suffered a truly human death! Jesus experienced fully every human emotion.

He experienced helpless infancy, parental nurturing and maturing in family life. During His earthly ministry, He experienced friendships with His disciples and human desperation as those who sought healing approached Him. He experienced hunger, thirst, weariness and worry. He also experienced anger and frustration when He drove the tax collectors from the temple (see Matt. 21:12).

In the end, He also experienced unwarranted persecution, pain and finally death. But, more than just the physical pain, He experienced emotional pain. It was part of the purpose of His coming in human form. On the cross He exclaimed, "My God, my God, why have

You forsaken Me?" (Matt. 27:46b; Mark 15:34b NKJV). He was not forsaken; He was being allowed to experience an emotional pain that we often feel.

God gave His WORD not just as a token (like some politicians posing for a photo), but to demonstrate to us that He fully understands, feels and knows just how we feel in any given circumstance. This is the *why*.

## CHAPTER FOUR

# God's Preparations

Anytime someone has an idea, then thoughts and planning ensue. That idea may then become a project, such as some home improvement, a garden, or other. Preparation is next, and everything for the project is made ready. At least, that is how most things proceed. Of course, there are those times when there is little thought or preparation behind an idea.

For example, someone may see a hungry, cold, stray dog and suddenly decide to rescue him. Once home, the dog stays. That was likely a spontaneous decision with no time for strategy or much preparation. Something like that can lead to disaster, though, because there was likely no thought regarding where the dog would sleep, what to feed it once home, what to do with it when away from home at one's job, etc.

I was one of those people who faced this very scenario. Once many years ago, I awoke one morning and, as usual, strolled out onto my patio. Only this time I noticed a small white clump in my small yard near the base of the fence. I thought it was a piece of old cloth or perhaps a paper cup that had blown into the yard. As I walked over to pick it up,

I realized it was not a piece of cloth or cup, for I could hear the sounds of a tiny kitten and noticed it moving a bit.

There had been a feral cat coming around regularly to eat food and water I put out for her. I reasoned that this obviously newborn kitten must be hers. Of course, I vainly searched to see whether I could find the mother cat or where her other kittens might be so I could return this one.

Outside was damp from a light rain with a temperature of about 50 degrees, so the kitten was cold and wet. I took it inside temporarily, thinking the mother cat would return for it. It was likely only a couple of hours old, so the mother cat must have given birth in my yard and then moved the other kittens, accidentally leaving this one behind.

I had no food for it and no place to keep it, and I wondered whether the mother would even return. I had seen the mother cat every day, but not that day. Everything was interrupted. I needed to find a place for the kitten, get cat milk from the pet store, and do what I could to keep it alive until its mother returned. As one might imagine, this was definitely not a planned event or occurrence!

I fed the kitten every three hours and kept it warm and comfortable for the next three days until the mother finally appeared. However, by the time I had retrieved the kitten to return it to her, she had vanished once more. I saw her again a few days later, but, believing she would reject the kitten, I continued feeding and caring for it. I was preparing and planning as things went along. The kitten grew, thrived and stayed.

The point is, most people who want a pet will have thought about it, made plans, prepared accordingly and then obtained the pet they decided upon, whether from a breeder, pet store or local animal shelter as the last act. They will have already acquired food, bedding and supplies and made the appropriate arrangements.

Even putting in some new plants or planting a garden is done after thought, plans and preparations. No one who thinks about mowing the grass will even go outside to do so unless he or she has a working lawn mower and gasoline for the mower. We can't walk outside thinking a mower will just suddenly appear.

### God Is a God of Preparation

Our God is not a God of coincidence or accident. He conceives, plans, orchestrates and delivers. It is no wonder why, when God created all things, He first called forth light, saying, "'Let there be light,' and there was light" (Gen. 1:3 NIV). Thereafter He separated land from water and created plants of all kinds; He created stars, planets, sea creatures, land creatures and the Garden of Eden.

His last creation was a human man, Adam, and then Eve, as a wife for Adam (see Gen. 1 and 2). Some wonder why God didn't create man first, since He made man to rule over the earth (see Gen. 1:26). I believe it was because God wanted to put in place everything that humans would need to thrive and multiply. Had He created mankind first, then there would have been nothing for food, shelter, light or other necessities for survival. I believe God already had the idea for man, had thought of everything necessary, and then began implementing the plan methodically, thoroughly and completely before placing man on earth.

We see that our God is not a god of thoughtless actions. Since He knows all, He won't act haphazardly, leaving anything to chance. It is not to say that, despite all of God's perfect efforts, we, as humans, don't bring about difficulties. God has given us free will that, when used according to His purposes, results as He desires and, when used otherwise, can result in disasters.

Also, it is not to say that God cannot "fix" any situation. In fact, God can and does bring about good even from bad or unfortunate situations (see Rom. 8:28). I believe He particularly delights in thwarting Satan's sabotage. We can and do stray from His divine plans; however, there is nothing God cannot do (see Luke 1:37). He can bring about His desired result regardless.

Of course, man is above the animals and is not a "pet." But we are still God's creation, as are all things. However, we are unique as we were created in His own image (see Gen. 1:27). Nothing else was created in His image, and nothing else was given charge over what was created previous to mankind. So, of course, God made us special; He did so knowingly, purposefully and after careful preparation.

We were not an afterthought. How amazing that He thought, instigated, planned and prepared especially for us! He made the seas, land, plants and creatures of every sort. But, each creation also was thoughtful and in perfect order. He made us perfect also.

### No Detail Overlooked

I'm certain there is no one among us who hasn't thought about a project, made plans, prepared and then, partway through the implementation, realized we were lacking something necessary to complete that project. All of us have experienced the discovery of a small detail we had not anticipated or thought about ahead of time.

I remember in the Christmas movie, *National Lampoon's Christmas Vacation* (1989), starring Chevy Chase, when he takes the entire family into the woods to cut their own family Christmas tree. After tramping through the snow for a time and finally finding a suitable tree, the son asks whether they remembered to bring a saw. Since they had not, the next image shows them driving down the highway with the tree on top of their automobile, roots and all!

There are times in our lives when we overlooked something that, in retrospect, seemed so obvious that it is ludicrous to realize we forgot. Often, and thankfully so, we are able to remedy the situation and continue on with little more than inconvenience. Sometimes we overlook something serious.

During World War II, my dad and the soldiers in his company were marching toward a forward position to engage the enemy. Partway through their march, they were allowed to stop for a brief rest. My dad sat beneath a tree and hung his issued bandolier of ammunition on a limb. After their brief respite, they continued their march, and as they neared the enemy position and readied themselves for imminent combat, my dad suddenly remembered that he'd left his bandolier of ammunition hanging on the tree! This could have been a fatal mistake.

I know there are times we think God has forgotten us, especially when we find ourselves in difficult or even terrible situations. The Israelites found themselves between the Egyptian army and the sea! How frighteningly impossible things must have seemed.

However, as Gabriel told Mary, there is nothing impossible with God (see Luke 1:37 NKJV). If He brought us to a place, as He most certainly did with Adam and Eve, then He most certainly made provisions. We will see exactly how He provided even beyond this life.

I've often heard the Alexander Graham Bell quote, "Preparation is the key to success."1 Benjamin Franklin famously said, "By failing to prepare, you are preparing to fail."2 I've noticed through personal experience that preparation will take longer than the ultimate act, but it ensures the desired outcome.

When putting myself through graduate school, I did handyman work, maintenance work and small subcontracting jobs involving anything from painting to carpentry. Before I could begin painting even a single room, I had to tape it off, lay drop cloths, remove faceplates from the walls, move furniture, remove doorknobs and fill holes.

After all the preparations were completed, only then could I open the paint cans to begin the actual paint application. In every instance, the preparations took far longer than the actual act of painting. But, once preparations were complete, the remainder of the work moved much faster.

I often saw the sloppy results of previous work, with paint on hinges, doorknobs, outlet covers and windowpanes—obviously someone's paint job hastily done with little regard for careful preparation. There is never anything wrong with being thorough.

A certain doctor's patient complained about the time his doctor was taking. The doctor replied that when he was younger and in school, he was often criticized for being "slow." The doctor remarked how he preferred to think he was just being thorough. The patient later realized the importance of the doctor's careful, methodical and deliberately unhurried approach. When it's life or death, being thorough won't be criticized!

Some may wonder why God took six days to create everything, including man. After all, God is infinite with unlimited power. Remember, though, that God's timing is always perfect; His answers are always best; His plan is infallible; and His preparations are always thorough. His WORD was not sent by accident.

## CHAPTER FIVE

# The Consequences of a Mistake

Whenever an idea, thought or plan begins to eventually become reality, a great many details reveal themselves that may not initially have been pertinent, relevant, present or observed. Sometimes these missed details are a direct result of our own failure to plan thoroughly, of human error or our own neglect.

Other times, things surface that complicate or become problematic due to no fault of our own. Nevertheless, to successfully complete the project, the problems that surface must be addressed. Ignoring a problem simply delays the inevitable failure of the project, makes futile our effort, or guarantees its ultimate demise. Disregarding instructions is the usual reason for failure.

When God created our world, He created the Garden of Eden, which was in the east. God made trees grow from the ground, and in the middle of the Garden of Eden were two trees: the Tree of Life and the Tree of the Knowledge of Good and Evil (see Gen. 2:9). He then placed Adam (and later Eve) in this garden (see Gen. 2:8).

Upon placing Adam in this garden, He informed Adam that he was free to eat of any tree in the garden, but he "must" not eat from the Tree of the Knowledge of Good and Evil. If he did, then he would "certainly die." (Read Genesis 2:15–17 NIV.)

### "Don't Eat It"

Whether Adam and Eve had a concept of death or not is an interesting detail for discussion. They were the first humans and thus had not experienced death, dying or debilitating health or even seen such among other creatures. But, for the sake of argument, we might assume that God allowed them to understand the concept of death and dying as opposed to life and living.

God informed Adam that he "must" not partake of the fruit from the Tree of the Knowledge of Good and Evil. God could have ordered him not to even go near the tree besides informing him that he "must" not eat its fruit or even placed an angel to guard this tree and its fruit. By informing Adam that he "must" not eat of this fruit or he would die, God was giving man free will.

God could have made it impossible for man to eat of this fruit by preventing access to the tree. He could have made it impossible to reach the fruit, which could have grown only from the highest, most inaccessible limbs, or He could even have allowed harm to occur from an electrical force field or other barrier were one to even approach the tree to within a certain distance.

God "advised" Adam about the fruit of this tree and informed him of the results should he not heed the admonishment about what "must" not be done. I remember when my son Daniel was a toddler, I would warn him of things to keep him safe. Small children have little concept of certain types of danger, although they do understand pain and fear.

We went to a pizzeria one evening and on the table were the usual items, including a salt shaker, a Parmesan cheese container, and a large red pepper flake dispenser. At his age, Daniel was curious, wanting to explore everything. This is a common behavior of children his age, and it is how they learn about the world around them.

I was always encouraging because I wanted to see him learn, experience and explore the wonder of all around him. The only things off limits were things that I knew would be harmful or unsafe. In those instances, I would try to explain how something would be harmful.

This evening, however, he ignored my warnings, including my explanations that the red pepper container he continued grabbing would hurt him. After taking the container from him three times, each time admonishing him that it contained hot pepper, I realized that he was going to continue. He was in the "terrible two" age bracket, so this undoubtedly had something to do with his insistence.

I could have removed the container from the table. Instead, I decided that if he grabbed the container again, I'd simply let him learn on his own about hot pepper. Naturally, as soon as I left the table to retrieve our pizza order, he grabbed the hot pepper container, managed to open the top, and got hot pepper flakes on his hand and in his mouth.

I noticed what had happened as well as what happened next. He immediately realized he wanted nothing more to do with the hot pepper and began gulping cold water as sweat poured from his forehead. I cleaned his hands while I explained again that hot pepper would burn him.

Sometimes experience is the best teacher. He never forgot that unpleasant experience, and from then on, if I needed him to avoid something harmful, all I had to do was mention "hot pepper," and he instantly ceased whatever he was attempting. All my warnings, explanations and requests were ignored; his own painful experience communicated far more and produced the desired result.

In the Garden of Eden, Adam and Eve had choices because God had given mankind free will. I am certain that God wanted Adam and Eve to follow His advice because He already knew the consequences of eating fruit from the Tree of the Knowledge of Good and Evil. Unfortunately, the consequences were far more serious than my son's ingesting red pepper flakes at the pizzeria.

### Persuading Eve

Many of us have read the passages introducing us to the Tree of the Knowledge of Good and Evil thinking God admonished both Adam and Eve about the dangers of eating of the fruit of the tree, but biblical passages tell us that God informed only Adam that he must not eat from this tree. We know this is so because, when God advised Adam, Eve had not yet been created (see Gen. 2:15–17,22).

We also see an additional clue in Eve's rendition of God's admonishment to the serpent; she said they were not to eat the fruit of this tree or "touch it" (Gen. 3:3–4 NIV). According to the wording of these passages, it isn't clear if Eve was stating God admonished against touching the tree or the fruit of the tree. So, I believe it is a fair implication that Adam must have informed Eve about the tree, since Eve could not have been present when God informed Adam because she had not yet been created.

The Bible doesn't recount details about how Eve actually obtained a fruit from the tree; we don't know whether the serpent actually handed it to her or whether she plucked it from the tree herself. Of course, had the serpent removed one of the fruits from the tree to hand to Eve, she would have instantly seen that touching it did not kill the serpent, so perhaps this obvious detail would have been additionally persuasive.

God had never told Adam that merely" touching" the fruit or the tree would bring death, though, and likely the serpent knew this, so handing Eve one of the fruits was a clever way of luring her into a false sense of security. At that point, the serpent would have certainly appeared more credible.

All the serpent had to do was convince Eve to take one taste. Since Eve was holding the fruit harmlessly in her hand, it certainly must not have seemed dangerous, so whatever the serpent told her must have sounded even more convincing.

A seriously interesting part of this passage is the fact that the serpent talked (see Gen 3:1–5). In no other place in Genesis does the Bible recount any other creature being able to speak. When Eve touched the fruit and felt no pain, she must have wondered, *How bad can it be?*

When my son Daniel held the container of hot pepper flakes, it certainly hadn't harmed him. It seemed innocent enough. But, as soon as he went further and tasted some, the harm came. Eve tasted the fruit and didn't die; she found the fruit "good for food" (Gen. 3:6a NIV). She gave some to Adam, who also ate of it (see Gen. 3:6).

I am certain that when Eve offered Adam some of the fruit, he could see that she had not died, and he likely doubted God's warning. Then their eyes were "opened" (Gen. 3:7a NIV). For the first time since God created them, they became aware of evil. Innocence ended, fear entered their lives, and they no longer had access to the Tree of Life (see Gen. 3:10,22–24).

I believe a good many people who may have read through these passages wondered why Adam and Eve didn't die after consuming the "forbidden fruit." God never said they would die instantly, as one might reasonably expect to happen upon ingesting a deadly poison. He informed Adam that he would die, and, indeed, Adam did die a mortal death (see Gen. 5:5).

Had Adam never consumed the forbidden fruit, he would have had access to the fruit from the Tree of Life in the Garden of Eden. He would never have known evil, his spiritual self would have remained pure; he would have been able to remain in the Garden.

## Making the Wrong Choice

Throughout our lives, we are confronted by any number of temptations and any number of things that are purportedly harmful. My own dad contracted lung cancer, eventually dying after enduring much suffering. When he began smoking cigarettes early in his life, I believe no one knew the potential dangers. Later, when various studies and medical science declared cigarette smoking to be harmful and potentially deadly, he, and a good many others, continued smoking.

I heard comments along the lines of, "If it's so bad, why hasn't it hurt me?" I've never heard of a single cigarette killing anyone or of anyone dying instantly upon finishing a package of cigarettes. However, although I know of an extremely few instances of individuals smoking daily into old age, this does not happen to the vast majority of smokers.

There are various substances that can and do cause death; some kill almost instantly, such as some snake venoms, while others such as arsenic, mercury or radiation eventually cause death with symptoms not instantly apparent.

In life, once we become aware of something, we are able to make a choice about it. If we don't know of a thing existing, we cannot choose that thing. Facing too many choices often leads to confusion, possibly choosing wrongly, and the diminishing likelihood of choosing correctly.

Everyone remembers those dreaded "multiple choice exams" from school where, out of four choices, one only had a twenty-five percent chance of selecting correctly. We all have made wrong choices, been tempted and been faced with too many possibilities simultaneously. All have faced the consequences of having made a wrong choice. Sometimes, and thankfully so, a wrong choice doesn't have lasting, punishing or fateful results.

Guessing wrongly about which line at the store is likely to move along the quickest will, at worst, only delay our completing our purchasing. Taking a wrong turn on a trip may mean we go miles out of our way.

Greed adds to one's vulnerability to succumbing to temptation, which adds to the possibility of an incorrect selection. There is an old saying that if something appears "too good to be true," then it is indeed too good to be true! I'm sure we all have heard about someone being told that he or she won a prize but have to deposit "good faith" money for some reason to satisfy the purported prize source, only to later learn it was all just a scam. A "smooth talker" has parted many a victim from his or her money.

Adam and Eve had everything in the Garden of Eden; they had plenty to eat and all of God's best. They had no actual need for the fruit from the Tree of the Knowledge of Good and Evil. The serpent was the original "smooth talker."

Imagine Eve encountering a creature, clearly not human, that could actually talk. That alone would be quite astonishing! Being able to engage in reasoning and being able to exhibit and demonstrate seemingly accurate information, while casting doubt, all worked against Eve.

Eating of the forbidden fruit meant that Adam would die a natural, mortal death; it also meant that his spiritual relationship with God was forever flawed. He now knew sin and evil, became aware of adverse morals, was no longer pure, and could no longer reside in the Garden of Eden.

He would eventually die outside of the Garden, a place where no human would ever set foot in again. Furthermore, no human would ever have access to the Tree of Life because God sent cherubim and a flaming sword to guard the tree (see Gen. 3:24).

God's loving arrangements for mankind were forever altered. Knowledge of evil includes not only the knowledge of harmful things, but also the ability to choose immoral, harmful ways and things that go against God.

Man would now have to toil and experience pain and death. Now all manner of sin could interfere with human existence. As we shall discuss later, God would again intervene, directly impacting humanity following inappropriate behavior. His WORD was to come.

Jude tells us that "the only God our Savior" is the only One who can present us "before his glorious presence without fault," through Jesus Christ our Lord, "before all ages" (Jude 1:24b–25 NIV). We read further in Revelation how John sees Jesus and is told, "…I am the First and the Last. I am the Living One; I was dead, and now look, I am alive forever and ever…" (Rev. 1:17b–18 NIV).

"…I am the Alpha and the Omega, the Beginning and the End" (Rev. 21:6a NIV; see also Rev. 22:13). Remember how we discussed that "in the beginning was the *Word*" (John 1:1a NIV, emphasis added). This passage further illustrates how the WORD was the beginning of all, existed first and will exist in the end and forever.

## CHAPTER SIX

# Temptations Cause Problems

In the Garden of Eden, the serpent was both a distraction and a cause of temptation. When the serpent talked to Eve, I can imagine how distracting and surprising that was. Eve succumbed to the temptation, as did Adam. Now, Eve could have simply walked away and checked in with God about the "forbidden" fruit or even mentioned to Adam what had happened so Adam could consult God. However, she didn't.

Satan will always use our weaknesses against us, whether that weakness is an old habit such as smoking; childhood trauma; old wounds reopened to revisit the pain upon us; or some other issue. He cannot physically attack us directly, so he will use us against ourselves. Regardless, he gets the desired result: preventing us and depriving us of something God intends. Adam and Eve could have lived in the Garden of Eve forever but for their succumbing to the serpent's temptation.

We all have and will face temptations throughout our lives. A candy bar right now might satisfy an empty stomach, but that small, sweet taste won't last long. Nor will it replace a meal with real protein and vitamins. A smoker trying to quit thinks "just one last cigarette" won't hurt a thing, except the "last" one likely isn't the last one after all. An alcoholic's sobriety ends when taking "just one" drink as a "reward" for remaining sober for a time, thinking there's no harm.

Along another line, enduring another's chiding, criticism, teasing, taunting and mockery just to win that person's approval won't ever end future criticism. One will never get that person's approval, either! All that the needy one experiences is manipulation, control and low self-esteem.

Success often means resisting the immediate urge, whether it is to satisfy a craving, stop ridicule or obtain release. The key to success is persistent consistency, focus and effort. Nothing happens overnight; instead, endurance wins. The way to endure even the harshest temptations is through God's strength. He won't give up on us if we don't give up on Him! We've all heard Vince Lombardi's saying, "Winners never quit, and quitters never win."1

### The Halfway Mark

There is a beginning, a middle and an end to all things mortal. No one would begin swimming across a lake only to get halfway across and decide it's time to quit. Quitting means drowning. Halfway across means there's only halfway to go. How far anyone has come proves what can be done.

Just because we're still working towards a goal does not mean it's out of reach; it only means we're not there yet. There will be times when we may think there's still a long way to go when, in reality, we've already come a long way. Effort wasted is a goal unmet. In the middle of the lake, just one more stroke means we're already more than halfway across.

In my years of running marathons, I have found that reaching mile fourteen is special, since it means I'm already more than halfway done. Then, I anticipate reaching mile seventeen because, by then, the distance to finish is only the distance of three 5K races.

During some marathons, I saw runners ready to quit after reaching mile twenty. I have actually seen a few runners simply sit down on the curb, thinking they couldn't go any further. The truth is, after running twenty miles, the worst is over; with only six miles left, it is not the time to quit.

Often a little encouragement at that time is all that's needed. There have been times when God allowed me to be in the position to offer that encouragement. God always knows what we need, how to deliver it, and when. I remember helping someone up off the curb and telling him I wouldn't let him quit and would run the remainder of the way with him.

In simpler terms, none of us goes to the grocery store with a list of items to purchase and buys only half the items on the list. Only after we have everything on our list do we check out and return home. Who would want to get home with only half the necessary items and be unable to prepare the meal?

No one wants to have to return to the store immediately after arriving home. We all know how that feels—getting home only to realize we forgot something. Forgetting is human, but no one leaves without everything on his or her shopping list on purpose.

When Jesus healed a blind man, He didn't just return sight to one of the man's eyes! If we're painting a wall in our house, we wouldn't paint just half of it and quit! Doing anything only halfway means it is not done. Just before Jesus died on the cross, He stated, "It is finished" (John 19:30a NIV).

Jesus finished all that He came to accomplish. Otherwise, we would not and could not have eternal life, and our plan for salvation could not be accomplished. Prophecy would not have been fulfilled. God never does anything halfway, so it was necessary for Jesus to be crucified and experience death.

In life we may proceed with a task incrementally for one reason or another, which in some cases makes a particular task seem less daunting. There's nothing wrong with completing a series of steps to complete the whole. Painting only one room at a time in our house may be easier to manage than tackling the entire house all at once. Staying consistent will see the project finished.

During my educational years, I operated a small painting contracting business. It was always easier to paint if the area to be painted was empty because, after preparation, the paint could be applied rapidly. However, painting my own home always required doing only a room at a time because the furniture had to be moved out of the way.

One of the main reasons we might not begin a project is that we allow ourselves to feel overwhelmed. That feeling is all too familiar, for Satan can use it as a distraction to prevent us from even trying. Little can be done in the spirit of fear.

The greater the seeming enormity of a project, the greater the likelihood it won't get done or perhaps even started. In such circumstances, breaking the project into small steps will make completion seem more achievable. Anyone who has ever restored a vintage automobile knows the phrase "a work in progress."

Our lives on this earth are a work in progress. We have a beginning, a middle and an end. We may hasten our own end, or we may have a different ending by succumbing to a temptation that derails our progress or diverts our efforts. To stay the course, stay with God.

## Make Your Life Count

Distractions are a very subtle form of temptation. Most of us think of temptation as giving in to something, but we fail to realize that a distraction tempts us away from our focus. Almost everyone can remember a time when a little encouragement went a long way, and we reached our goal.

We also can remember a time when others around us discouraged us through criticism, subtle innuendo or detraction. We should never listen to discouragement and detractions from others because, if they have time to distract and detract, then it's a guarantee they have strayed from the course somewhere in their own lives.

Those who offer encouraging words are God's messengers sending us hope, strength and moral support, reassuring us that we need to stay focused and continue on in order to reach our goal. We all will face discouragement, obstacles, setbacks and interference. God has never promised things would be easy.

He may very well make some things easy, but if He does not, even difficult things are always possible with God. True, complete, absolute, unwavering faith can move mountains or let us walk on water (see

Matt. 17:20; 14:29). Temptations distract and lead to failure and even blindness. Samson's succumbing to temptation led to his downfall and being blinded (see Judges 16:21).

The Lord's prayer includes a request to "not lead us into temptation, but deliver us from the evil one..." for a reason (Matt. 6:13 NKJV). Jesus knew we all will face temptations; He also knew evil would try to distract us through any means necessary, including temptation, to prevent us from achieving all He planned for our lives.

This life lasts only once; whatever we do during this lifetime will be with us until death. Moreover, things we don't do will also be with us until death. There's nothing worse than a lifetime of regrets. Make life count!

There are times in life when we face unbelievable or impossible situations. We all will face some unknown or previously unanticipated situation. Our human knowledge, discernment and wisdom are lacking in those cases. A hasty decision invites regret.

Indeed, a decision made in panic, fear, ignorance or indifference is often wrong. We will be the one paying the price for that decision. Whether that "price" is nominal or leads to greater problems than previously existed, in retrospect we might wonder, "How could I have been so stupid?"

In facing temptation, we have choices. We can succumb to the temptation; resist it, avoiding it for the moment in order to delay a decision until a later, clearer, calmer or more knowledgeable perspective prevails; or repel it entirely. Besides these three choices, we always have a fourth option: we can seek God's direction and strength. God will always provide a "way out" so we can endure any temptation (see 1 Cor. 10:13).

When Christ was in the wilderness fasting, Satan tempted Him in several ways. However, Christ relied upon scripture to not only resist Satan, but also to overcome (see Matt. 4:1; Mark 1:13; Luke 4:2). Christ's example—of relying on scripture and biblical truths—is likewise available to us when we face temptation.

As we will discuss in Chapter Ten, "the prayer of a righteous person is powerful and effective" (James 5:16b NIV). I have heard some comment that they don't believe God will hear their prayers because they are unworthy. However, God hears all prayers!

God knows the number of hairs on our heads; He knows all the stars by name; He knew us before we were born; and He knows even when a sparrow falls (see Matt. 10:29–30; Ps. 147:4; Jer. 1:5). It is simply impossible that God does not hear every prayer. Anyone praying sincerely not only will be heard, but also will have his or her prayer answered according to God's will. Although there are few guarantees in this life, I humbly guarantee that God will, without any doubt, hear your prayer!

In working to complete this book, I have had to "'pray my way" through completion. Quite often I felt I didn't have adequate words to convey the message I believed God was leading me to convey. However, He always supplied the material according to and in all the ways I believed were His direction.

Upon completion of my master's degree, I received a very prestigious, beneficial job offer from a state agency that would have allowed me to begin my career after having just completed my degree. That same week I also received an acceptance letter from a very good out-of-state law school. I couldn't do both, since attending an out-of-state law school would prevent my accepting the job offer and remaining in Texas.

Regardless of my choice, it would be life-altering. The job had wonderful benefits, a good salary and a great retirement plan. Law school was no guarantee, since many freshmen law students do not survive beyond that first year. Law school would require up to a three-year commitment; it had no benefits and no promises; it meant struggling financially and still undergoing a job search after hopefully graduating. Many might have advised me to "take the money and run!"

I knew God had the answer, and I would trust His decision. Although neither choice would necessarily be wrong, both would affect the entire direction of my life. Extremely few are given the opportunity to attend law school. Law school wouldn't necessarily preclude a similar or even better job offer than the one at hand. However, accepting the job offer would preclude becoming a lawyer.

I knew that declining law school, never obtaining a law degree, and never becoming a lawyer would be something I'd regret for the rest of my life. The reader can see from my bio which choice I made. I never had any regrets. God's will never causes us regrets. He will never tempt anyone with anything wrong, though He may very well allow temptation to see our resolve or to bring us to Him in prayer. His direction is never incorrect.

### Persevere

God has never promised things would be easy. In fact, many times we face difficulties wondering, as Jesus did, about being forsaken. We discussed at the end of Chapter Three just how Jesus knows this feeling! Just because we cannot see our future or understand why something is happening in the present does not mean it is without purpose.

I believe that when we endure difficulties, we are being prepared. As a marathon runner, I didn't just wake up one morning and think I would go out and run twenty-six-plus miles. My running began with shorter distances before I eventually ran my first marathon in February of 2011.

Running longer and longer distances and training for that first marathon was not easy. It was grueling, time-consuming and painful. However, without going through the difficulties of training, I would not have been able to complete that first marathon.

Life is not unlike a marathon. Life requires perseverance, effort, dedication, patience and difficulties along the way. This is why we are told, "Let us run with perseverance the race marked out for us" (Heb. 12:1c NIV).

When facing any temptation, first and foremost consider how the decision or action will glorify God. Ask yourself, "Will my service to Him be more or less effective?" Other considerations to contemplate include these:

1. What will be the natural result of succumbing to the temptation?
2. Will following the temptation impact or prevent something that would not otherwise be?
3. Will my present choice permanently eliminate a different choice?
4. Am I simply choosing the path of least resistance?
5. How will or might my choice affect other things in life or the future God has in store?

6. Will my decision result in something illegal, immoral or wrong, or all of them?
7. How will succumbing to the temptation affect others?
8. Will my present decision impact my future for better or worse? Will it result in lifelong regrets?
9. Will a wrong decision preclude correction without consequences?
10. Will the decision only resolve something immediate or something of greater concern that will be permanent if not addressed?

No matter how we proceed in life, we only get to do life once. Whether we do it "right" or not has no effect on the certainty of its ending. We all face mortality, and only those who believe will see Jesus. Only then can we know every reason, every purpose and all the answers to our most important questions. Jesus has the answers and is the answer.

He was before time; He voluntarily came here for us; and He returned to the heavenly realm to receive us there. God gave His WORD, which was His best gift because our salvation is guaranteed. How then can we do less than our best for Him? He is waiting for us to join Him and be with Him forever.

## CHAPTER SEVEN

# Starting Fresh

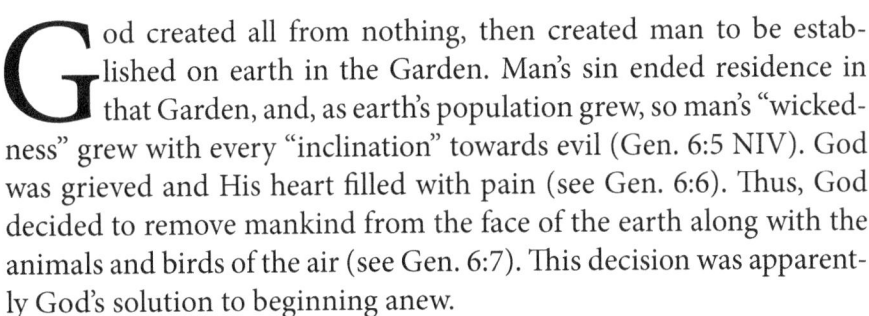

God created all from nothing, then created man to be established on earth in the Garden. Man's sin ended residence in that Garden, and, as earth's population grew, so man's "wickedness" grew with every "inclination" towards evil (Gen. 6:5 NIV). God was grieved and His heart filled with pain (see Gen. 6:6). Thus, God decided to remove mankind from the face of the earth along with the animals and birds of the air (see Gen. 6:7). This decision was apparently God's solution to beginning anew.

### Remove the Old Before Building the New

Often, before we can begin a project, whether it is building a house or a commercial structure or even planting a garden, we must first remove any current or offending obstacles. Sometimes we remove unpleasant things because they remind us of unpleasant memories or our own procrastination, neglect or oversight. The old saying of "out of sight, out of mind" illustrates this thought.

If we want to erect a new house, then a proper foundation will be needed before we can erect the new structure itself. Usually, the land must be cleared and all debris removed since it may not be feasible or possible to build around any obstacles. If there exists an old, dilapidated structure, it will have to be removed. We are constantly involved in tearing down and rebuilding. Sometimes a thing has simply outlived its usefulness.

God decided that every creature that had the "breath of life" in it would be destroyed by a great flood (Gen. 6:17a NIV). However, Noah had found favor with God, and the scriptures state that Noah was righteous among the people of that time (see Gen. 6:8–9). So, God allowed Noah, his three sons Shem, Ham and Japheth, along with Noah's wife and the wives of his three sons, to escape the destruction to come (see Gen. 6:18).

God planned for Noah to preserve a pair of each living animal to restock the earth following the flood (see Gen. 6:19–20). Although many believe only two of each animal were saved, the Bible clearly reveals that seven of every kind of "clean" animal and two of every "unclean" animal, plus seven of every kind of bird, were rescued from the coming flood (Gen. 7:2–3).

Following God's instructions, Noah built a great ark to protect, house and preserve his family and the animal life (see Gen. 6:14–17). This great flood, which covered the earth with water for 150 days, "destroyed" every living thing on the face of the earth (Gen. 7:23–24 NKJV). Humans, animals, birds and other creatures were "wiped out" (Gen. 7:23a NIV).

God intended to cleanse the earth from wickedness. We use water to wash our bodies, our clothing and our food. God was washing the entire earth to cleanse it from human corruption. The sinful ways of mankind, the interbreeding among human women and "sons of God" (thought to be fallen angels), every thought of evil "all the time," and every manner of vile, immoral, depraved, corruption possible was to be eliminated (Gen. 6:4–6 NIV).

God gave mankind another chance by wiping the slate clean and allowing for a fresh start. It was like tearing down an old structure with the intent of rebuilding in its place something new and better. Before God would replace, He first had to remove.

No one would remodel a house by building a second story on a structure that was termite-infested, with crumbling walls, a deteriorated foundation and obnoxious odors emanating from the first floor. To do so would be foolish and a waste of time and resources and would only add to the misery of the first floor.

God, the great Architect of the universe, knew this all too well. He created all, and as no master builder would simply build on a debilitated structure, neither would God. He removed the bad before starting over with the good.

The flood destroyed every living creature save those in the ark. There was to be a fresh, new and uncorrupted earth. The flood was the involuntary cleansing of the earth. No one was free to choose to enter the ark; only those God selected were able to enter. Noah was a direct descendant of Adam. God preserved humans with Noah and his family.

As discussed earlier, God had given Adam and Eve free will; they could select anything suitable for food in the Garden of Eden, but God told Adam he "must" not eat of the fruit from the Tree of the Knowledge of Good and Evil (Gen. 2:17a NIV). When Adam and Eve ate its fruit, sin came into the world. Sin never left the world because every human descended from Adam and Eve.

God undoubtedly knew that even though He had cleansed the earth from the wickedness existing before the flood, evil and sin would still arise. However, perhaps He was hopeful that, with a fresh start, mankind would realize His power and a large enough number would remain faithful to goodness, so following in the footsteps of Noah.

### A New Way

The flood clearly demonstrated that God can take away at any time all that He has given. Sometimes setting an example is the only way to gain compliance. Perhaps, and quite often, it does have that effect, but as we see in today's society, it is not completely successful. Although God declared He would never again bring a flood upon the earth to destroy everything, He did have another way of cleansing sin (see Gen. 8:21).

Christ Himself would have to come into the world to cleanse mankind with His very own blood. Of course, Christ saw everything the Father saw because "in the beginning was the Word, and the Word was with God, and the Word was God" (John 1:1 NIV).

Christ knew the world would not be forever devoid of sin. He also knew that, although the flood removed all but what was saved in the ark, sin had entered the world through man and would remain. But He also knew, though floodwaters cleansed and removed the offending involuntarily, that His blood would be all that could cleanse completely so mankind would again be able to experience the presence of God.

Christ would sacrifice Himself for man to be able to enter heaven and reside with God. It would be the only way. However, there is a great difference. For the flood, God did not allow anyone to choose whether to be drowned or saved. God deliberately saved Noah and his family; no one else received the invitation to be saved in the ark.

However, through Christ, we *all* have the invitation to be saved and live forever beyond the grave of our earthly lives. Christ came that we might "have life, and have it to the full" (John 10:10b NIV). Christ was "the light of the world" (John 8:12a NIV). Christ told His disciples that He was "the way and the truth and the life" (John 14:6a NIV).

Perhaps, after reading this passage, the reader understands that we can choose Christ as our savior, which is clearly what God intended in sending Christ to redeem the world. But, beyond this, we must also understand something about the Tree of Life that was also in the Garden of Eden. God tells us in the Book of Revelation that the Tree of Life is with Him (see Rev. 2:7; 22:1–3). The implication might logically be understood to mean that God saved the Tree of Life before the flood by removing it from the Garden of Eden so that man might still be able to partake of its fruit. However, only through Christ does man have the ability to access everlasting life.

In reading Revelation 2:7 and 22:1–3, we are clearly informed that the Tree of Life is in paradise with God, and it grows on either side of the river of the water of life. So, upon God's bringing the great flood to destroy humanity and all life upon the surface of the earth, He intentionally preserved not only Noah, his family and certain animals and birds, but also the Tree of Life.

The river of the water of life flows "from the throne of God and the Lamb" (Rev. 22:1b NIV). The Bible never indicates that God removed the entire Garden of Eden to paradise, only the Tree of Life. The Garden of Eden was a real place on earth with biblical descriptions giving us an idea of its location; it was where Adam and Eve originally lived until they were banished from it (see Gen. 3:23).

I believe that those who accept Christ will be able to access the Tree of Life, still. The Book of Revelation tells us, "Blessed are those who wash their robes, that they may have the right to the tree of life…" (Rev. 22:14 NIV). When the Tree of Life remained in Eden, God had a cherubim and a flaming sword guarding it. However, now that it is in paradise with God, there is no further need for a guard.

Further, Christ came to redeem the world so that, through Him, mankind can once again access the Tree of Life. We must first "wash our robes" before we can become blessed with eternal life. "Robes" refer to a covering or clothing. Man did not use clothing until after partaking of the fruit of the Tree of the Knowledge of Good and Evil (see Gen. 3:21). Afterward, mankind was covered with sin, which must first be washed clean before we have a right to the Tree of Life. Christ washes us clean through His blood that was shed for us (see 1 John 1:7).

The flood was meant to cleanse the earth of wickedness, but mankind's sinful nature would still ever make us unworthy to dwell with God. The only way mankind can enter into eternal life is through Christ. But, unlike the flood when God brought destruction and mankind had no choice in survival, we now have free choice to accept Christ or not. Now He brings destruction upon no one. Instead, our option allows us entry into the city, having free access to the Tree of Life.

God deliberately saved the Tree of Life for us, if we want it. In the beginning, He said Adam must not eat from the Tree of the Knowledge of Good and Evil or he would die. This was telling Adam what not to do; however, now God tells us what we should do to have eternal life.

I am certain that, if we are given a choice, we will choose something good over something harmful. Had I placed a slice of pie on the table next to the pepper container at the pizza place, my son would have chosen the pie and left the hot pepper alone. Of course, he would first have to believe that the pie was better tasting than the hot pepper.

We still have a choice: either Christ and life everlasting or not! God loves us and wants us with Him forever. Because He loved Adam and Eve, He was surely hurt and angry by their failure to heed His warnings. He had given them a choice to eat of the fruit from any plant or tree in the Garden of Eden except for one: the Tree of the Knowledge of Good and Evil.

Temptation interceded, intent on thwarting God's plans. However, the serpent completely underestimated the WORD that was God. We may very well make wrong choices during our lifetime, whether through our own ignorance, through a mistake or as a result of temptation. Choosing Christ is never a mistake or a wrong choice!

CHAPTER EIGHT

# Our Future Protected

God conceived a plan, then prepared thoroughly, implementing in the smallest detail all that would work together according to His will for His creation. Nothing was forgotten, missing or an afterthought; nothing would escape His thoughtful gaze. His implementations included ordering day and night, separating sky from expanse, separating water from water (I believe saltwater from fresh waters), and establishing seasons.

It is quite extraordinary that He would go to such lengths with such careful and thorough preparations for man. As I ponder this scenario, it is with wonder, but also delight, knowing we meant so much to Him. No wonder we call Him "Father," for only a loving father would extend to his children so much care, provision and abundance.

### We Will Make Mistakes

There is an old adage in the world of law used by attorneys in trial work: "A bell cannot be unrung."[1] This saying refers to something being said in court, in front of the jury, that perhaps the jurors should not have heard. In other words, once the jurors hear what was said, they cannot unhear it. Once something is done, it cannot be undone, though perhaps there are times things can be corrected.

A car I once owned received some damage that required body work and then substantial painting to conclude the repairs. When the body shop called and informed me the car was ready, I went to pick up the vehicle and settle the repair bill.

The first thing I noticed was that the shop had used the wrong color of paint. The body work was great, and the paint application was flawless. However, the color used was clearly wrong. Apparently, they had ordered paint according to a guide for a newer model of the same vehicle, which did not match correctly. Of course, they corrected the problem by using the right paint color.

Fortunately, we are able to correct a good many mistakes in life. In correcting our mistakes, we can learn from them, but things cannot be "undone." My great-grandfather was a truly skilled carpenter and cabinet maker. My grandfather was an amateur wood worker, and he'd learned something from his father (my great-grandfather) that he taught me: "Measure twice and cut once."

No human is infallible. There are times we will make mistakes, forget things, not plan thoroughly and be less than prepared. Fortunately, in perhaps most instances, we can correct a mistake without irreversible consequences. Of course, there may be times in life that we did something mistakenly that resulted in permanent consequences.

Imagine hunting and mistakenly killing someone's horse, thinking the brown color moving in the brush was a deer. That is a terrible mistake with permanent consequences, since the horse cannot be brought back to life. As a young man, I took my two kid brothers hunting one afternoon. They both learned a valuable lesson that day when one of them could have gotten shot by the other!

In our lifetime, we will continually make mistakes, face difficulties and encounter others also making mistakes and having problems of their own. Fortunately, God forgives our shortcomings and our failures and will usually give us a way to correct our mistake or make things right to whatever extent possible.

Making mistakes is human. Continually making the same mistake is both foolish as well as frustrating to those around us. Making amends is one of the most valuable human actions we can take. It's easy to forgive others' mistakes when they admit wrong, face the consequences or problem, and then do their best to set things straight.

The Bible tells us to forgive, and we will be forgiven (see Luke 6:37). Proverbs tells us that "...whoever heeds correction is honored" (Prov. 13:18 NIV). In other words, if we make a mistake, recognize it and pay attention to correction, we will be respected.

If we remember those times in our lives when someone made a mistake, but then, after realizing the mistake, admitted it, apologized for it, and did his or her best to correct matters, those around that person tended to remember the strength of his or her character rather than the details of the original mistake.

However, there are also those who, for whatever reason, will never admit wrongdoing, mistakes, thoughtlessness, cruelty or flaw. Those around them will know them for these traits, will not respect them, and will have as little to do with them as possible. "Whoever hates correction is stupid" (Prov. 12:1b NIV). This description is indeed strong criticism.

Of course, we wouldn't want to surround ourselves with such people because being around them is like being around toxic substances. We all know those types of people who take a toll on us just by being around us. We feel stressed, irritated, on edge, anxious, fatigued and perhaps even fearful. Just being close to an atomic blast is destructive!

### God Planned in Advance

God leaves nothing to chance and works everything out for His own ends (see Prov. 16:4). He created the heavens and the earth, the flora and fauna, together with all living things. It was all according to a plan, and therein were careful, considered, thoughtful, complete, detailed preparations.

Imagine bringing home a dog from the local animal shelter and then releasing it into the yard without giving thought about food, water, shelter, care, training, or its life under our ownership. We discussed in Chapter Four our creation after God's meticulous preparations of a place for mankind with all we needed to survive and even thrive. But, He also made "forever" provisions of a future life beyond this earth.

Imagine being invited and sent a complimentary ticket to a prestigious event in another city in another state or even country. You know you are expected to attend, but you have no way of getting there and no place to stay once there. Not only would this situation make you feel anxious and frustrated, but it would also feel impossible.

Imagine a soldier being sent on a high-level mission with provisions for getting there, instructions on how to achieve the desired results, and every asset necessary for successful accomplishment, but no instructions, provisions or means of return afterward.

To the soldier, this signifies a "suicide" mission. He (or she) is not expected to return whether he fails to successfully prevail or actually accomplishes the mission. He's expendable, and, regardless of success or failure, he will have no hope of survival.

Had God created all things with this type of scenario in mind, then we would have absolutely no hope either. A good life or evil life would result in the same end. We would never make it "home." However, we are not expendable to God. He wanted us home, so He did the only thing He could to ensure this result: the WORD became flesh.

A sense of duty; a belief that his (or her) actions will benefit his loved ones, humanity or his country; or perhaps a belief that his sacrifice will earn him fame, respect or even the satisfaction of revenge may be what drives the soldier onward to accomplish his mission. The reasons propelling him forward may, or may not, be realistic. Whatever his own unrealistic, irrational or even delusional beliefs, they won't matter once he's gone!

We all have experienced times when we thought we'd planned and prepared, but then had second thoughts. Perhaps we've even had an idea and planned strategically how to implement and complete the project, only to find upon nearing completion that we had some important afterthoughts.

There's the common saying that "hindsight is 20/20."2 Likely no one has ever finished a project that, by the time it was completed, he or she had not learned a better way to have completed it or decided how to proceed differently if it is ever again undertaken. We cannot see into the future, and we often cannot anticipate certain events or obstacles that may come our way.

World travel is more common today than at any time in history. Millions of people travel by air daily, whether for pleasure or work. Those who travel for work likely are in and out of airports every week, catching flights to every point imaginable. Those individuals likely have their "routine" down solid.

However, some people may only travel once annually for vacation or other intended pleasure. They may not have the "routine" down, but they may plan and prepare as much as possible to avoid longer lines through security, avoid unnecessary delays such as baggage search, and allow sufficient time for changing planes.

However, neither of these two groups of passengers, regardless of their best efforts, could anticipate a hijacking or a crash. I have yet to see a passenger bringing along his or her own parachute in the event of some type of disaster.

It should be completely reassuring that God not only knows every possible scenario but also has planned for it, making perfect arrangements for the "now" as well as for the future. He didn't just create us and then turn us loose on this planet, hoping for the best. He actually made it possible for us to have the best.

Moreover, He planned and prepared not only beyond the future in this form of life, but also beyond any life we can imagine. By first creating both the heavens and the earth, then establishing a "kingdom" that would never end, ultimately making us a part of it all, we can know His arrangements, plans and preparations with every detail perfectly wrought than we presently observe.

## CHAPTER NINE

# Trust God's Truth

God is infallible, perfect in every way, and completely reliable. Thus, His promises can be relied upon and will always be fulfilled. A promise by God is a promise kept. Just as a word from man cannot be unspoken, neither can the word of God be undone or unsaid. As the old saying goes, "A man's word should be his bond."

In today's world, someone's word may be worth little, with promises being easily forgotten. In the Book of Hebrews, we read of Christ being the fulfillment of Old Testament prophecy (see Heb. 1). In other words, He is God's promises delivered. "He who promised is faithful" (Heb. 10:23b NIV). God is trustworthy, faithful and dependable. God does not lie! (See Titus 1:2.) God's promise brought His WORD to "light" (Tit. 1:3a NIV). By His promise we can receive eternal life (see 1 John 2:25).

**Broken Promises**

Humans are fallible, can be forgetful, are sometimes unreliable or irresponsible, and other times can be quite careless. Despite even our best intentions, we can fall short. A promise may go dormant for an inordinate amount of time due to procrastination. Some matters beyond our control, such as illness, accident, catastrophe or personal distress, may interfere with fulfilling our expressed promises.

In making a promise, the one to whom it is made relies upon it as our word. We all have heard about the "check being in the mail." If someone is really in dire financial circumstances, that reassurance is thin. Imagine waiting for someone who promised to pick us up at the airport but who never appears. We'll understand if we later learn that person was involved in a car accident on the way to the airport.

Imagine a small child being promised something by a parent, only to be disappointed when the parent doesn't come through. Once is likely forgivable, but a pattern of habitual failures causes disappointment that is never forgotten. Unfulfilled promises were common in my dysfunctional family.

Everyone can identify with having received someone's promise over something certain, but later nothing happened. We have also experienced receiving a promise that, due to the inordinate passage of time, we finally realized would never be fulfilled.

In my law practice, the client always received my best representation. I cared about my clients' problems and genuinely wanted to help them. However, in a few cases it was always disappointing to favorably conclude a client's legal work, quite often obtaining far better results than expected, then realizing, due to the passage of time, I would never be paid.

A broken promise can lead to mistrust, disappointment, frustration and even the destruction of a relationship. Even when a promise can't be kept through no fault of the one making it, disappointment and perhaps even frustration will likely result, depending on the importance of the promise.

Such a situation won't likely lead to blame or even anger, but nonetheless is still disappointing. I remember contracting for some cabinetry work and remodeling to be done at our home. After beginning the work and completing a small portion of it, the contractor had a paralyzing stroke, ended up hospitalized, and then, while in the hospital, had another stroke that was fatal.

I was disappointed because his work was of such wonderful quality that I knew it would be difficult to find another of his level of skill.

However, I attached no blame to him, and though I was disappointed, I also felt badly for his family.

In a family situation, children learn from their parents, other family members, friends and their societal environment. Children, especially very young children, depend upon their parents for necessities, comfort, nurturing and love. Children growing up in a dysfunctional family will learn that broken promises are the norm rather than the rarity.

From the ever-occurring broken promises, the child will learn not to trust the offending parent. That distrust will become pervasive throughout the child's life even into adulthood, unless it is finally and completely remedied. Not only will the child not trust any promises that the parent makes, but he or she won't believe much, if anything at all, that parent says.

In other words, that parent becomes unreliable and untrustworthy, which leads to the destruction of the relationship. It also can foster a type of emotional trauma that may affect the child long into adulthood, perhaps affecting his or her ability to trust anyone or, far worse, leading him or her into believing it is acceptable to lie, deceive and break a promise.

Keeping one's word, to the extent we have control over the circumstances involved, is one of the most important things we can do and teach our children. Not only are we demonstrating our reliability, but we also are reinforcing the importance of keeping one's word. We also benefit from keeping promises because a good reputation is priceless. Without a good reputation, nothing else really matters.

### You Can Depend Upon God

Reliability is key in any relationship. No one wants a friend who can never be relied upon. No one wants a spouse who can't be trusted. No one wants a parent who is a disappointment. The difference among the three is that we can choose our friends and our spouses, but we don't get to pick our parents. We have no control over parents who aren't decent, honorable and responsible.

Our God is reliable! His WORD is a guarantee! God chose us, planned for us, provided for us and prepared for our futures. We can trust anything and everything He says. Even when we don't understand His answer, we can know His way is best for us, ultimately.

We may feel disappointed over something at the moment, only to later realize that momentary disappointment was a blessing in disguise. God said to Jeremiah, "For I know the plans I have for you... plans to prosper you and not to harm you, plans to give you hope and a future" (Jer. 29:11 NIV). He is a good, faithful and loving Father.

Jesus taught the disciples the "Lord's Prayer," and a portion of that prayer asks that God's will be done (see Matt. 6:10). We cannot know God's will in every circumstance, although we can know His will is for good. God is neither evil nor a liar. What we can know is that we can trust, rely upon and be thankful He is taking care of us, even when we don't realize it.

Nothing He does is irresponsible. He will never forget a promise, and there is nothing that can prevent His promise from being fulfilled. We can know with absolute certainty that we can trust Him in all things. There are no circumstances beyond God's control. He won't take back His word, change His promise or try to explain anything away. He never has to "justify" anything or make excuses. God does not play games!

There will be times in this life when we won't understand why something happens. However, we must realize that there will be times when we aren't supposed to understand. But, remember that God knows when we don't understand and why we don't understand because our ways are not His ways (see Isa. 55:8). However, His ways are perfect and loving (see 2 Sam. 22:31; Ps. 25:10).

I suppose one of the most usual situations of not understanding is when a child doesn't understand why his (or her) parents are taking him to the doctor when they both know the doctor will administer an injection or inoculation that may be a bit painful at the time. The parents know the treatment will prevent a potentially deadly disease. The child only knows something painful is about to befall him.

We, as parents, already know about the dreaded disease that we hope the necessary treatment will prevent because we have likely seen the devastation the disease brings. Also, no loving, right-thinking parents would knowingly allow their child to ingest poison.

In this lifetime, God has protected us from a good many "poisons." Whether we realized it at the time or not, perhaps the thing we thought we wanted was something God already knew would not be the best for us.

There may have been a job we didn't get, even though we really thought we wanted it and thought it would be a perfect fit. Perhaps a relationship, for some reason or other, just didn't work out. Or perhaps even something so simple and inconvenient as a detour on our way to work kept us from a terrible accident.

Before buying my first house, I thought I'd found something affordable that would be a good purchase, only to learn that it was already "under contract." Initially, I was disappointed, but I soon found another house that cost less and was bigger, newer and in a better neighborhood. Had I not been prevented from purchasing the first house, I would not have gotten the better place God intended for me.

God always wants the best for us. We should never "settle," whether in a relationship or in a search for a home, a job or other need. Jesus told the disciples, "Which of you, if your son asks for bread, will give him a stone? Or if he asks for a fish, will give him a snake?" (Matt 7:9 NIV). He reminded them that if parents know how to give good gifts to their children, then "how much more will your Father in heaven give good gifts to those who ask him" (Matt. 7:11b NIV). God gave us His WORD; nothing could be better.

If we don't interfere, God will always give us His best, for He knows exactly what we need, when we need it. Of course, if we are stubborn about having our way, then we may, indeed, receive far less than what He had in mind.

If we don't get a particular job, God must have had something better waiting. He knows the talents, abilities, personalities and interests He gave us. He not only gives us His best, but He also expects our best and will put us where He needs us. I believe He delights in seeing us use the gifts He gave us in a place where we can use those gifts to His greater glory.

CHAPTER TEN

# Prayer Is Effective

W e are not to "be anxious about anything, but in every situation, by prayer and petition, with thanksgiving, present
your requests to God" (Phil 4:6 NIV). "The prayer of a
righteous person is powerful and effective" (James 5:16b NIV).

Anyone who has ever done any gardening or planted seeds must
wait for them to sprout and grow. No one can expect to eat the fruit
the same day one planted the seeds. It doesn't work that way. Farmers
till the soil, fertilize it, plant the seed, then wait for the harvest. They
can do all in their power, but they still must wait for God to cause the
seeds to grow.

When my children were young, I made up a story for them about
two farmers. Both prayed and asked for God's blessings. One farmer
tilled the soil, fertilized it, planted seed, irrigated the crops and worked
the land every day while the other sat on his porch staring into his
fields without doing any work. The second farmer exclaimed that God
didn't need his help and could make a crop grow regardless.

The one who worked his land was blessed with a bountiful crop,
while the other farmer's land grew nothing but weeds. The man who

had not worked didn't understand why he received no crop, despite his faith that God was all powerful and could do anything, including causing a crop to grow.

## We Must Do Our Part

In the Book of James we are told that we "do not have because [we] do not ask," but it goes on to tell us that we must ask with right motives (James 4:2b–3 NIV). I honestly believe that God expects us to do our part. If He gives us work to do, we must do it to the best of our ability. "Whatever you do, work at it with all your heart, as working for the Lord, not for human masters" (Col. 3:23 NIV).

I don't believe God expects us to do something only He can do. He doesn't expect the impossible of us, but He does expect us to give our best efforts. If we undertake something we believe He has led us to do, He will bless our efforts and see us through. Our motives should not be selfish, arrogant, boastful, greedy or lazy.

God will not do our homework and will not do any of our other work. He has given us work to do and expects us to do it. There is no greater waste than for someone who has been given a great talent but refuses to use it. My children understood that I was telling them that "God helps those who help themselves."

Any parent can remember how it felt, after giving children certain chores around the house, to later learn the chores went undone. The parent's frustration was the understandable result of the child's irresponsibility. Chores are given to children to help them learn, to become aware of responsibility, and to help them grow.

I believe chores also help children in the development of their self-esteem. A chore successfully completed results in feeling a sense of accomplishment. Any right-thinking parent wants his or her children to grow physically, mentally and emotionally. The parent also wants the children to know the feeling of accomplishment, the satisfaction of a job well done.

No one among us wants to feel like a constant and chronic failure. And, certainly, no one among us wants to be made to feel this way, either. Success leads to success. However, failure can also lead to success, so long as we decide not to let failure win. We must also realize that, as humans, we can give our best human efforts and do everything right so far as possible and still not succeed. But even when we don't reach our goal, achievement still occurs.

## Struggle Produces Strength

Jabez did not pray for an easy life. He asked God to bless him, expand his territory and keep him from evil (see 1 Chron. 4:10). It is not selfish to ask for God's blessings but rather courageous, for we can never know just how God may choose to bless us or in what form the blessing will take. Also, we can never know just how God will expect us to use that blessing.

Jason Padgett was attacked one night and seriously injured, but apparently, as a result of the injuries he sustained, developed synesthesia, making him an "acquired savant." His brain injuries reportedly caused internal alterations, which, in essence, resulted in his becoming a mathematical genius.[1]

I'm certain that none among us wishes to be nearly killed; nevertheless, imagine becoming so seriously ill and near death but eventually surviving. We may not know the purpose for our struggle and pain, but perhaps because of what the doctors learned in caring for us a new treatment was discovered that might be used to save others.

Also, God does not harm us. Evil brings harm, and God is not evil. However, regardless of what harm may befall us as a result of evil, God can bring good. "Do not pray for an easy life," said Bruce Lee, "pray for the strength to endure a difficult one."[2]

Jesus explained to His disciples how to pray and gave them the "Lord's Prayer" (see Matt. 6:9–13). The key, I believe, in prayer is praying God's will, which is always the correct motive. Of course, God understands every mental state, every concern and even our immaturity. He is forever, and our level of maturity, even as adults, will never reach a supernatural omniscience.

We know that the prayer of the upright pleases God (see Prov. 15:8). James tells us that "the prayer of a righteous person is powerful and effective" (James 5:16b NIV). In other words, God is pleased when we pray according to His will because, in so praying, we are trusting Him, knowing He will always do what is best for us.

Imagine praying for God to make us rich beyond our wildest dreams, only to be permanently injured and confined to a bed for what little life we may have left, yet incredibly wealthy because of the monetary damages we received as a result of the act that injured us.

We should be careful because wrong motives in prayer will not benefit us. There is an old saying from Aesop that says, "Be careful what you wish for, lest it become true." There are some things we must endure in order to grow.

Anyone who has ever tried to ride a bicycle knows that falling is a part of learning how to ride. We can't learn to ride without getting on the bike and we can't learn to swim without getting in the water. We aren't born with the ability to walk, and before we learn, we'll have stumbled and fallen any number of times.

This life is a process, and the more we learn, the farther along we are in the process. There will be times we stumble, times we fall and times we just can't move. Those times we don't think we can is when we're accepting defeat.

Bruce Lee also said, "Defeat is a state of mind."3 Indeed, if we think we are defeated, then we are. I believe when life hurts, we should pay particular attention to what we can learn from the situation. God may allow some frustration, some failure, some pain and some struggle, but never with an evil intention.

Remember the caterpillar entering its chrysalis (cocoon), then emerging as a beautiful butterfly? When the butterfly is emerging, it must struggle and strain to remove itself from that small enclosure wherein it has been confined for the time necessary to transform into a butterfly.

You have probably heard the story of someone helping a struggling butterfly out of the chrysalis. The person freed the butterfly, but it couldn't fly. The purpose of its struggle was to strengthen the butterfly, so once out it would have the ability to spread its wings and fly. By releasing the butterfly and bypassing the struggle, the person deprived it of a way to acquire enough strength to fly. Thus, that butterfly could never be all it was intended to be.

God has created us for a purpose. We weren't a mindless creation, an afterthought, an accident. Sadly, some individuals may never know their purpose. They may never acquire what was necessary to become all that God intended them to be.

Struggles, pains, discomforts, inconveniences and difficulties strengthen us, causing us to develop beyond what we are and allowing us to become all we can be. God has given us enough, but He also has given us free will. Too many choose the "easy way" out rather than praying for courage to endure the hard way.

"And my God will meet all your needs according to the riches of his glory in Christ Jesus" (Phil. 4:19 NIV). Ephesians 3:20 (NIV) tells us that He is "able to do immeasurably more than all we ask or imagine, according to his power that is at work within us." Paul even infers that suffering produces character in Romans 5:3–4. No human has lived without experiencing some pain. It is our nature to try and avoid pain, as is true among all living things.

Even if we didn't look forward to some pain, we would choose pain if necessary. However, we would not deliberately choose pain under most normal, ordinary circumstances. Having been a runner since my law school days earning my doctorate, I have often described running as the exercise I "hate to love."

Having run more than 200 full marathons, some ultra-marathons, and many shorter races, I can attest to the pain involved in running distances. In fact, most exercises involve some endurance and some amount of pain. And, as we have discussed, even beginning to learn how to ride a bicycle usually involves some painful experiences.

Exercise enables muscle growth; mental exercises enable learning; and prayer strengthens our relationship with God. We learn, grow, expand, mature and become better versions of ourselves. The caterpillar that became a butterfly couldn't fly without struggling first to free itself.

Many times life has us in a confining situation, and it is by struggling free of that confinement that we become more than we thought possible, as well as all we were intended to become. It is prayer during these times that enables us to call on God's strength, when ours isn't sufficient alone. Our strength is limited, but God's is not.

## CHAPTER ELEVEN

# Why Should We Pray?

I have often heard people commenting that if God already knows all things and knows everyone's needs, then why is prayer necessary? The Bible tells us that "the prayer of the righteous pleases [God]" (Prov. 15:8b NIV). Moreover, Philippians 4:6 (NKJV) tells us, "…in everything by prayer and supplication, with thanksgiving, let your requests be made known to God."

These and other passages suggest that not only does prayer please God, but also (I actually believe) that He *wants* our interaction with Him. Some say they don't want to "bother" God since He has much more important things to attend to than whatever they might have to say. I assure everyone reading this book that God is never too busy to listen, is never bothered by our prayers, and is more than able to attend to everything.

### God Wants Our Attention

There was a time when, as a child, I wondered whether God was too busy to listen. I decided there were more important things going on than what was happening in my life. It concerns me today that there are still people who feel this way. Nothing is further from the truth.

God does know what we need, when we need it, and how to satisfy that need. Even when we don't ask, even when we don't know, He is working for our good. Our Father knows what we need before we ask (see Matt. 6:8).

Those of us with children often realized what things our children needed before they did. We knew everything they needed for their first day of school and for sports, and we knew how to comfort them when they were sick.

Imagine, if we as human parents can know and see to these things, how much more God is able to provide. Jesus tells us that the Father feeds and cares for the birds, which neither sow nor reap, and we are even more important to Him (see Matt. 6:25–26). He can and He will!

Even though we realize that He knows what we need, we may still struggle with why, then, we should pray. I believe the answer is much simpler than we might imagine. We don't have to have a long, elaborate prayer before we get God's attention. It simply isn't necessary. (See Matthew 6:7–8.)

However, in prayer, we are deliberately focusing on God and on communication with Him. During our day, we might be so involved in our activities that we aren't very focused on Him and would likely miss something He might be trying to convey.

But in prayer, we have made a conscious decision to focus our attention away from all else but God. It is then that He has our undivided attention like we always have His undivided attention. We open ourselves to receive whatever He imparts. We also become closer to Him, which is what He desires above all else.

Having raised children, I remember trying to do several things at once in caring for them. I'm quite certain the counterperson at McDonalds needed a great deal of patience when trying to understand my order as I attempted answering my children's incessant questions and figuring out what they had now reconsidered ordering to eat while also being interrogated about the toy of the week.

There were times I simply had to ask the counterperson to "hold that thought," then turn my full attention to my children and explain to them that what they needed to tell me was very important, so for me to hear it all, I needed to finish ordering so they would have my full attention.

Using this technique let them know they were important; what they wanted to tell me was important to me; I didn't want to only give them a little of my attention, but all of it; and they weren't being ignored.

When my children asked something, I knew they needed a response. I knew I needed to give them my full attention so I could give them a complete answer, rather than just dismiss them. It always comforted them to have my full, undivided attention, to hear everything on their minds. It also let them know that they mattered and their needs mattered.

They also realized that I was always there for them, to listen and to hear them out, and that they could always come to me about anything. As parents, we should always want that from our children: For them to know they can always come to us about anything and everything. There is a confidence in that knowledge, a reassurance of understanding rather than abrupt dismissal.

God will never dismiss our prayer as nonsense, minor, inconvenient or even ridiculous. He wants to hear us, and He wants us to know that. Marathon training involves hours of running long distances, and some have asked if I listen to music or talk on my cell phone to keep from being bored when I'm doing my training runs. I tell them God is a great listener; I don't need music—I pray.

### Give God Gratitude

In prayer, I thank God before anything else. Perhaps God enjoys hearing how we noticed even those small things He continually does for us on a daily basis that, in our human condition, often go unnoticed. Perhaps He wants to know we appreciate Him. But, as much as anything, He will know we understand the attitude of gratitude.

We read in the Gospel of Luke how Jesus cured the ten lepers who called out to Him from a distance. He told them to show themselves to the priests, and as they went, they were cured. All continued on but one who, when he saw he was healed, returned to thank Jesus. (See Luke 17:12–15.) There is no doubt that anyone being cured of leprosy would have been profoundly appreciative, but only one expressed gratitude.

There are lessons to be learned in this story: thanking someone takes little effort but means much to the one thanked; it never hurts to say "thank you"; and thanking someone demonstrates gratitude. We can know the effect of a simple "thank you" from hearing one of our children telling us how much he or she appreciated a gift we gave, something we did or how we helped the child.

By the child's thanking us, he or she is learning thoughtfulness. With so much "entitlement" in society today, more thoughtfulness and less selfishness would go a long way. By expressing gratitude, we are also learning to focus on the good.

In my years as a practicing attorney, I handled all manner of cases. I believed in "giving back" and would take court-appointed cases. Many times, regardless of how much time or work I invested in a court-appointed client's case, rarely would a client even bother offering a "thanks."

It seems such clients' attitude was, "Why should I thank you for doing your 'job'?" Also, quite often, it was clear from their attitude that I would never be able to please them. I could never have done enough, and whatever I did was never good enough. Although frustrating, it was during those times I was satisfied knowing that I was doing the job I believe God had called me to do.

No matter what, we can never thank God enough for all He has done, continues to do, and has arranged for all eternity. We can live our entire lives in gratitude for all the ways God blesses us, and it would still not be enough. He has done what no one else could do by coming into this world just for us.

There is no way we can ever be deserving of this perfect act of love. He still did so, knowing there would be some who would still refuse to believe, some who would still be ungrateful, and some who would outright deny His existence.

There will be times when we pray out of desperation. Other times we will pray for a miracle. Then, there will be times we pray out of happiness, joy and prosperity. Life contains all these and more. Every life has had tragedy, desperation, hurt and disease, but also happiness, prosperity and joy.

Regardless of our present circumstances, we can and should pray. It is easy to pray and thank God during good times; it is harder to rejoice in God's blessings during struggles, pain and tragedy. God is the same, though, whether we are happy or hurting.

He still wants to hear from us and always hears our prayers. Even when we pray and His answer is "no," He is still working for our benefit and blessing. An answer of "no" might be painful at the time, but it will be the correct answer because He already has things worked out according to His will for good (see Rom. 8:28).

Regardless of our present circumstance, in prayer we can know that "peace of God, which surpasses all understanding, [which] will guard your hearts and minds through Christ Jesus" (Phil. 4:7 NKJV). God wants communication with us; He wants our expression of gratitude so He feels our heart; and He wants us to feel the calm, the love, the care and the protections of Him, who is Father of all.

It is obvious that He wants us, or He would not have created us. Although He already knows about our day, hearing about it from us shows our thoughtfulness. Communicating with God through prayer sets our mind free, gives us an inner peace, and reassures us. He wants this because He tells us that whatever is true, noble, just, pure, lovely, or worthy, to dwell on these things (see Phil. 4:8).

In prayer, we are dwelling on Him, and there is nothing better, more lovely, more peaceful, more worthy or purer than God. Not only does He care about our physical needs, but He also cares about our mental, emotional and spiritual needs.

## CHAPTER TWELVE

# God's Surprises

God not only has miracles in the palm of His hand, but He also holds an unlimited number of surprises. When we pray, thanking God and asking for His blessings, whatever His response is, it is always for good and never for anything bad. He will never bless us with a wrong thing, although He may very well let us have our way, despite His best warnings.

Praying in God's will is the sure way to receive His blessings. Besides hearing our requests, He also sees the motive behind those requests. He knows our heart. King Solomon asked God to give him wisdom so he could properly and effectively rule. God was pleased with this request and granted it. (See 1 Kings 3:5–15.)

However, not only did God give Solomon wisdom, but He also gave him more than he asked, giving him riches, honor and a long life (see 1 Kings 3:12–14). As we read through these passages detailing Solomon's request, God noticed Solomon did not ask for wealth, long life or even for his enemies to be destroyed. Solomon only wanted to be able to serve God by being a discerning ruler.

Life will never present the vast majority of us with a situation requiring our governing a nation. Nevertheless, we will often need wisdom, discernment and strength in navigating this earthly life. We may face financial struggles, scheduling conflicts, health issues, parenting matters and other dilemmas. At no time is God unconcerned with our lives and at no time does He not understand.

### God Is Able

When we are faced with a difficulty or concern that we feel inadequate to resolve, God is able. At Bethsaida, the crowd of 5,000 that had gathered around Jesus to hear Him speak and to receive healing were hungry, but the disciples had only five loaves and two small fish, with no money to purchase additional food.

Jesus first offered a prayer of thanks for the five loaves and two fish, then all were fed, with twelve baskets of food left over. (See Luke 9:10–17.) The disciples had wanted Jesus to send the crowd away because they didn't have a way to feed them. I'm sure they felt overwhelmed when contemplating the seeming impossibility of feeding that many people. But God always has a way!

When thanking God for His blessings and asking for His will to be done, we should always be grateful for what we do have rather than focusing on what we don't have or weren't given. God will give us enough for anything He sends us to do. He won't abandon us after bringing us to a certain point, either.

If He brings us somewhere, He will see us through. Things may often look impossible, and I believe this is when God does some of His best work. How He must smile when His actions confound mortal man! The disciples must have been completely amazed after being able to feed everyone and still have twelve baskets of food left.

I'm sure all those men, women and children who were fed wondered where the disciples got all the food. I'm also certain God smiled in delight.

I've written before that, often, we ask for too little. God want us to have His best and wants to bless us completely. Jabez knew this and prayed accordingly (see 1 Chron. 4:10). We can't know the mind of God, but we can know His heart. His love and care abound. He delights in surprising us.

God not only gave Solomon the wisdom he requested, but He also surprised him with so much more. In asking for a raise, imagine how it would feel if the boss declined to give you the amount you requested because he thought it was too little and instead gave you double that amount!

We may ask God for anything, but He may not give us what we are asking for because He wants to give us something better. We can't see exactly what He has in mind because all we can see is what we know at the time. That is where our faith and trust come into play.

We should trust that He knows best and that, if we let Him, He will do even more than we expect or anticipate. More often than not, we miss out on everything God has in store for us because we decide we know better and insist on having our own way.

There are times when we pray over a situation and refuse to believe God's solution. In prayer, we cannot know just how God will answer, ultimately. At that time in that situation, He may say "no," not to deprive us, but to save us for what He really wants us to have.

If we refuse to listen or insist on having our way, we will certainly miss out on what God actually wanted to give us. That's when we shouldn't lament a loss but should be thankful we were spared what would surely have been a mistake or a less than desirable result.

If we think about it another way, imagine how God feels when He doesn't get to surprise us with our heart's desire because we failed or refused to trust His plan. Imagine insisting on having our way and never seeing what God had in mind!

## God Likes to Surprise Us

I believe that God delights in "surprising" us. We may plan, work and do everything in our power toward accomplishing a worthy goal while also asking for God's blessings in our efforts. We may anticipate every good result, feeling satisfied that we have done all we can do. Imagine, though, hoping for the best-case scenario that we might conservatively anticipate and receiving exponentially more.

I'm sure it was exactly this scenario when the disciples fished all night, catching nothing, and when Jesus told them to cast their nets on the right side of their boat. When they did, they caught so many fish they could not haul them into their boat! (See John 21:1–6.)

This result certainly was beyond their wildest imaginations. To use the word *surprise* is an understatement; I believe *astonished* and *amazed* more likely describes what was felt at that moment.

They had worked all night, were most certainly tired, very likely discouraged and probably just wanted to rest. Casting their net one more time was probably the last thing they wanted to do. Had they not done so, they would have totally missed out on the "surprise" waiting. God has surprises waiting, if we will just "let Him" surprise us. After all, who doesn't like surprises?

When my son was small, I would take him camping. The first time we went, along the way we stopped at a roadside rest area with picnic tables, trees and restrooms. After he used the facilities, he was running around playing and enjoying himself so much that when I told him it was time to go, he was upset.

He was having such a good time that he wanted to stay, camp there and play more. I tried to explain that our ultimate destination would be even more fun. I had been to the state park where we were going many times, but he had never been there to see how wonderful it was. All he knew was what he could see at that moment.

Of course, when we arrived, he had immeasurably more fun than he did at the rest area. I reminded him that had we simply stayed at the rest area, he would never have gotten to experience the place we now enjoyed.

Often, all we consider is the here and now, not realizing that things won't always be like the present because of our limited knowledge. Life has a way of developing, being modified through both internal and external forces, and changing for better or worse at times. Rarely does something remain the same.

We all age and mature, and, while as children we may think things will always be like it is presently, as adults we realize we've moved on from where we were, both physically and emotionally. Even as adults we must remind ourselves, especially during tough times, that things won't always be like the present.

Enjoy the present good times, endure those difficult times, antici-pate with eagerness even better things, regardless. There will be times when we must patiently endure, knowing the future brings promise.

There will be times we will want to never end, but we must sadly contemplate the most certain conclusion.

A tadpole lives in the two-dimensional world of water, yet, whether or not it wants to become a frog living in a three-dimensional world, it happens. The tadpole loses its gills and the ability to breathe under water, but it gains lungs for breathing air to allow living on dry land. The larva, or caterpillar, instinctively builds its chrysalis (cocoon), not knowing how long it will remain inside, what will happen while inside, or what will happen upon emerging.

God has surprises waiting that we cannot imagine! The caterpillar must surely be surprised at being able to fly after emerging from its chrysalis (cocoon) when, before, all it could do was crawl across the ground! Crawling along the ground limited what it could see of the world. But, as a butterfly, and now being able to fly through the air, it has a much different perspective. It could go further, faster, and experience far more than ever.

For now, all we can see is this stop along the way, and as wonderful as everything is that He created on this earth in providing for us here, there is nothing in our wildest imagination to compare with what He has ultimately waiting for us. He prepared this earth for us in this form of life. We can only anticipate all He has prepared for us in the next life! Regardless of what our minds can conceive or all we can hope, there is nothing to prepare us for the surprises God has waiting.

James 1:17a (NIV) says, "Every good and perfect gift is from above." Unlike the tadpole or caterpillar, we can know about the next life by knowing Christ and His divine assurances. Prepare to be astonished and amazed with astounding wonder!

CHAPTER THIRTEEN

# Have Faith

All of us have heard George Eliot's line, "Don't judge a book by its cover."1 Of course, a book's cover may attract our attention so that we want to see more, but what appears on the outside does not convey all that's on the inside.

One of the oldest books I have has a cover that is well worn, obviously old and a bit ragged around the edges, but inside the pages and illustrations are still in wonderful condition. When traveling, some of the best food I've enjoyed was served in a place that, from the outside, appeared to have seen better days, was run down and was obviously old.

**There's More Than Can Be Seen**

We are in this world of three dimensions. This is what we can see and what we know. If we look at a photo, we can only see what is depicted in that photo, but we cannot see beyond its borders. The photographer saw things outside his (or her) frame, and perhaps he even positioned his camera so as not to include certain things he saw that he didn't want in the photo.

When we stare at the night sky and see stars twinkling, we know they are stars, but—unless we are astronomers—we likely don't know their names, how far away they are, or what their surface might be like. We perceive only a part of what we see.

Anyone who has ever gone fishing realizes that there are fish in the water even though they cannot be seen. If we hear a dog barking, we realize it's a dog, whether we see it or not, but we may not know what breed it is. We can't see wind, but we can see its effect. We know what water is, even though it has no shape or form as a liquid but can become ice or snow.

Some believe because they have seen, but faith is believing in what we cannot see. "Now faith is being sure of what we hope for, being convinced of what we do not see" (Heb. 11:1 NET). I am certain that those who lived when Jesus walked this earth heard of miracles He performed. Many, and far more than the Bible accounts tell, saw miracles performed before their very eyes.

Quite naturally, Jesus' disciples observed more miracles than anyone else. So, of course, they knew His divine nature and had no doubt. They saw Him do things no one could do; heal people who could not be healed; and even return from the dead. We can only read biblical accounts of the many miracles Christ performed.

The Old Testament prophets foretold of Christ's coming and wrote of it. They believed God's promise regardless of whether they would ever live to see the fulfillment of that promise or not. It's easy to believe in something we observe. It is much harder to believe in something we've only heard about, especially if it is something so extraordinary that no one would believe it without seeing it.

I remember driving along a deserted section of a state highway one night during a rainstorm when something solid, something heavier than raindrops, began striking my car: small frogs were falling from the sky and hitting my windshield, my car hood and all over the pavement. Even seeing this phenomenon with my own eyes, it was hard to believe! I've never seen such a thing since, but what I saw that night was undeniable.

There are likely things we all have heard about that seem impossible, yet the source of the information is so credible, so reliable and so descriptive, we cannot discount its veracity. There are those occurrences we would call "awesome" or miraculous. Just because we cannot explain or understand something does not mean it didn't happen.

We are only able to explain or understand most things through our human senses. We understand height, depth, width and breadth. We also can experience taste, smell, sound, touch, temperature, pain, pleasure and emotion. We also have what some call intuition, speculation, "hunches" or a feeling we sometimes get in certain circumstances.

Many of our sensations can be felt and shared with others: whether it's hot or cold outside; how our favorite food tastes; or how wonderfully fragrant the flowers blooming in our garden smell. But when we tell someone, "Something just doesn't feel right," we can't get that person to also feel what we are feeling at that moment.

I've read of people with cancerous tumors observed on x-rays and verified with biopsies that somehow, before surgical removal, had completely vanish. Medical science could not explain how such a "cure" happened.

In my law office I had a screen saver on my computer screen that read, "The law has limitations; God does not!" Medical science can do much, but it still also has limitations. God does not. God Himself has given us great abilities, talents, resources, discoveries and all manner of life comforts. Yet, even with everything He has given and provided, He still has more.

As much as we can do, we are still limited. God is infinite, and nothing is beyond what He can do in any circumstance. Often, only when all else has failed do we then resort to prayer. We should pray first rather than as a last resort.

We must still do our part, but we should never make God an afterthought. He is always there waiting, willing and able. Pray first and last, first for His blessings and last in gratitude.

### Focus on God

We worry about the future and fret over a good many things that will never happen. Quite often anxiety occurs over unknown possibilities and unlikely scenarios. However, worry, anxiety, stress or apprehension are never productive. In fact, they are quite the opposite! Worry is a waste, as no amount of worry can change anything.

Instead of fearing the worst and immersing our minds in worry, we should consider positive thoughts that will affect our attitude and our ability to stay focused. God was and still is "in charge." Worry robs us of the opportunity to thank God for His presence in our lives, along with His manifold blessings.

Worry is Satan's way of distracting us from thinking on good things as we are directed in Philippians 4:8. There is a definite reason for this advice, for if we are thinking on positivity, we cannot think negatively. Our brains are not "wired" to think on the positive and negative simultaneously.

If our minds are filled with fear, apprehension and gloom, then we are unable to fully appreciate, focus on and be thankful for God's goodness. "Therefore do not worry about tomorrow, for tomorrow will worry about itself" (Matt. 6:34 NIV). Faith will always carry the day.

Jesus told Thomas, "Because you have seen me, you have believed; blessed are those who have not seen and yet have believed" (John 20:29 NIV). God has given us free will. He wants us to believe, to pray, to worship Him and to know Him.

Sadly, there are those who refuse to believe despite all. The question I always wonder is, just what would it take for them to believe? Would they had to have been there, when the angels appeared to the shepherds the night Jesus was born? Miracles don't just happen randomly.

Also, although there are those who may believe God doesn't exist because they didn't see the parting of the Red Sea or Jesus walking on water, the fact of the matter is that miracles occur every day. They come in all sizes, and a small miracle is nonetheless a miracle despite its not being something on the magnitude of the Red Sea's parting.

Once many years ago, while sitting outside on my patio praying, I suddenly felt something on my lap. Upon opening my eyes, I saw a dove on my lap. It didn't seem frightened, and, even though I began moving, it didn't fly off.

At that time I was still healing from some recent corrective surgery, and I was dealing with a number of other concerns. I couldn't explain this incident; it was something that just shouldn't have happened. Doves are not tame, and they are very wary birds, so I would never have thought it possible that one would actually land on my lap completely unafraid.

That dove came around frequently, allowing me to pet it, and would even follow me inside. Soon thereafter I had healed completely, and my other concerns were resolved. I felt that perhaps that miracle of the dove landing on my lap was God's message.

"So we fix our eyes not on what is seen, but on what is unseen, since what is seen is temporary, but what is unseen is eternal" (2 Cor. 4:18 NIV). God's WORD is eternal; He is from before time, through time and beyond time.

## CHAPTER FOURTEEN

# God's Grace Endures

No matter where we are in life and no matter what our past has been, there is no limit to God's grace. We cannot undo our past mistakes, but we can and should learn from them so as not to repeat them. If we continue making the same mistakes over and over, expecting different results, then we surely haven't learned anything.

At some point we either must change what we are doing wrong or give up. We either learn and enjoy success or refuse to learn and learn to fail. I'm grateful that God forgives our shortcomings.

### God Forgives All

Although God's grace is delineated throughout the Bible, the Book of Deuteronomy is dedicated to God's grace. In this book of the Bible we read how God will show His love to a thousand generations of those who love Him and keep His commandments (see Deut. 5:10).

During the entire time the Israelites wandered in the desert, He provided for their every need. Their clothing did not wear out; they were fed with manna; and they were given the Ten Commandments (see Deut. 8:3–4; 10:2; 29:5).

There were times when God was not pleased with the Israelites after their deliverance from Egypt. While Moses was on the mountain receiving the first tablets of stone containing the Ten Commandments, they prepared a golden calf to worship. God's displeasure at this extreme sin resulted in an entire generation perishing without entering the Promised Land. (See Exodus 32.)

Moses destroyed the first tablets, but God rewrote the Ten Commandments on two new tablets. Although God was displeased, He did not return the Israelites to Egypt, refuse to further provide for them, or discontinue leading them to the Promised Land.

Those same Israelites had seen the miracles that God performed, yet they failed to remain steadfast in their worship of Him. It does seem quite illogical to believe a statue of a golden calf, which they constructed, would have any power or be able to answer prayers. Man-made objects have no power over mankind; nor do they have any divine power at all. God created man; man did not create God.

We can be assured that God will forgive all of our mistakes, sins and wrongdoings if we repent and correct our actions. The first step towards repentance is recognizing that what we did was wrong, however. If we never acknowledge that what we did was wrong in the first place, then there is no true repentance.

Further, if we never recognize the wrong, then we may repeat that same wrong in the future. Mistakes, which we all make, are part of being human. We will continue making them, too (see 1 Kings 8:46).

Accepting that mistakes are inevitable should never excuse our failing to correct them. Mistakes can be a great opportunity for learning and growth. Forgiving ourselves after making a mistake, committing sin or engaging in wrongful conduct is often quite difficult.

Our God is gracious, loving and compassionate, though (see Neh. 9:17). He understands our frail human nature, and He extends forgiveness when we truly repent. True repentance is correcting our behavior and not repeating the same mistake.

### Release the Burden of Guilt

At times, our own guilt interferes with our self-forgiveness. I've heard people make the statement that God could never forgive them for something they perceived as unforgiveable. Some have lived through years of agony believing this lie.

Just imagine their daily distress in carrying this intense burden. Please remember that Satan is the father of lies! (See John 8:44.) If Satan convinces us that we are beyond God's forgiveness and extends our guilt, then we are unable to do our best in being all that God intends for us to be.

None of us is so powerful, mighty and above God's decisions that, even though God has forgiven us, we deliberately refuse to forgive ourselves. If we do this to ourselves, we are hindering God's purposes. We are also preventing or, at the very least, creating an obstacle to God's plans in our lives.

Guilt is a heavy burden. Guilt also can be healthy to an extent because it is evidence of our moral compass. Having no remorse or guilt over an obvious wrong indicates mental and emotional illness.

There are some who blame themselves for something they really did not cause but feel they should have prevented. One of my dad's best friends had a teenaged daughter who was killed in a car accident while she was on a date. The young man she was with that evening had too much to drink and shouldn't have been driving.

My dad's friend never got over his daughter's death. He blamed himself for letting his daughter go on that date. His way of dealing with his extreme guilt was to drink heavily every day, until he literally drank himself to death.

We may not have the strength to overcome certain obstacles, problems or overwhelming circumstances, but God has more than sufficient strength and power. He can reassure us in difficult times, during pain or when we face insurmountable opposition. He can do so even when it is us who are our own worst enemy!

The truth is that often we are harder on ourselves than others are. We often castigate ourselves, "punish" ourselves and treat ourselves worse than how we would treat someone else for committing the same perceived failing. God will forgive us, so if He does, why do we not forgive ourselves?

I'm certainly not suggesting that we forget our transgression, for otherwise we would not learn from it, However, forgiving and forgetting are not synonymous. We pray for others and extend understanding and forgiveness to them, so we should do it for ourselves.

There is no reason we cannot forgive ourselves. We must accept God's grace and let Him continue His good work in our lives. Our choice is simple: we can believe Satan's lies that tell us we aren't worthy of forgiveness, should be forever ashamed, and can never forgive ourselves; or we can accept the truth of God's grace, receive the inner peace that God's presence brings, and forgive ourselves so that we may continue in God's will.

There may be times when we don't want to forgive ourselves, preferring to wallow in self-pity, self-blame or self-loathing, but this is not what God wants. Remember, His will is supreme! We have free will to accept God's grace or reject it, but our refusal has a cost and consequences. His grace, though, costs nothing; it is free!

It is impossible for God to lie (see Heb. 6:18). When He tells us that He will forgive us and remember our sins "no more," we can believe Him and not carry a burden so heavy that we're unable to carry the responsibilities, perform the tasks, face the challenges and feel the satisfaction of being in God's will (see Heb. 10:17 NIV).

His grace covers everything, in all circumstances, for every condition and forever. It is a grace that is eternal, complete, timeless and perfect—*guaranteed!* He gave us His WORD, remember?

## CHAPTER FIFTEEN
# God's Love Is Forever

G od is love," says First John 4:16 (NIV). Love is mentioned hundreds of times throughout the Bible, perhaps because of its importance, its concept and its purity. I believe it is because, aside from Him, there is nothing God wants us to understand, experience and have more than love.

He tells us that He loves us and that He loved the world so much that He sent His only Son (see John 3:16). Through Christ, we can have and experience God's love forever, not just in this lifetime. Love, then, is so important that God wants us to have it always.

We love our children even when they make mistakes. They may do things we don't approve of and things we don't like, but nevertheless, even though we don't "love" something they did, we still love them.

We may even realize what possible temptations they'll face and know, almost with certainty, the mistakes they ultimately will make. We still love them. In the same way, God loves us regardless of our limitations, our fallibility and our ignorance. Fortunately, He is patient, kind and understanding. Throughout the Bible, especially in the Psalms, we are told that His love "endures forever."

### Love Is the Greatest

The great psychologist Abraham Maslow wrote of a "hierarchy of needs" that explained what we, as humans, need to survive and thrive.1 The most basic among these human necessities are our physiological needs, such as food and water.

As we continue reading Maslow's chart, however, we see that love is also a need. Some may argue that love is a wish, a hope or an option, but according to Maslow and others in the field, it is an absolute necessity. There is a difference between existing and thriving.

I once read about a German experiment in the thirteenth century that removed newborns from their mothers and confined them to a care facility where they were fed but never spoken to, caressed or touched by their caregivers. All of those babies died!2

Today, we would likely attribute their deaths to "failure to thrive syndrome." We are not meant to only exist; Jesus tells us that He came that we would have life to the fullest (see John 10:10). Anyone who has ever dealt with neglected children can tell the difference between those children and others who have had nurturing, love and care.

God loves us and demonstrates that constantly. The Bible reassures us: "His love endures forever" (1 Chron. 16:34 NIV; see also 2 Chron. 5:13; 20:21; Ps. 107:1; 118:1–4,29; 136). It wasn't enough that we would be reminded once; God tells us over and over that He loves us.

We, as parents, haven't told our children just once in their entire lifetimes that we love them; we have hopefully told them often. The word can never overused. There is no one among us who will tire of hearing that word.

I read in a humor column once about a man who said he told his wife when they got married that he loved her. When asked if he had ever told her he loved her since their wedding, he exclaimed "no"; he had told her that one time and hadn't changed his mind! Imagine if that were true?

The wonderful author and psychologist, Dr. Gary Chapman, wrote a very insightful book titled *The 5 Love Languages* (1992). In my family law practice, I often used his book and the quiz he created to determine someone's "love language."

I counseled many couples over the years, distributed copies of his book for them to read together, and used the information in his book to assist in evaluating marital concerns. Essentially, his book discusses and elaborates on five ways individuals show and receive expressions of love.

We don't just thrive on a singular expression or gesture of love. Everyone appreciates and delights in regular expressions of love, whether verbal, through physical actions, in thoughtful gestures, or another way. Of course, we should know our children or our spouses well enough to know what makes them feel our love.

Expressions of love are great, but sometimes our actions speak louder than words. I saw a scene on television of an obviously very surprised wife walking into the kitchen, seeing her husband washing all the dishes, and exclaiming, "I've never been more in love with you than I am right now."

God made us and knows each of us better than we know ourselves. He knows what makes us happy, what makes us feel loved, and, beyond that, what is in our best interests. Sometimes that is love—acting in someone's best interests whether that person understands it at the time or not.

Sometimes not getting what we think we want might just be a blessing after all! Our Father never wants to give us something He knows is not in our best interests. Sometimes what occurs may seem less than loving at the time, but it may be necessary.

Remember how Moses wanted to see the face of the Almighty? However, God knew that mortals could not behold His face without dying, so He placed Moses in the cleft of a rock so when God passed he would only see His back (see Exod. 33:22–23). It most certainly wasn't that God didn't love Moses enough to let him look upon His face; on the contrary, it was because God loved him enough to protect him.

The Bible tells us in First Corinthians 13 that, no matter how we proceed, what we do or what we have, without love we are nothing and gain nothing. This beautiful chapter of the Bible tells us about love never failing, being always hopeful and always persevering. We are told that of faith, hope and love, the greatest is love.

We began this chapter with the statement from the Book of First John that "God is love." So, it is logical, then, that love is the greatest because nothing is greater than God. Love overcomes any number of difficulties. Love even extends beyond the grave.

## Love's Legacy

Anyone who has ever planted a small tree knows that he or she will never live long enough to fully appreciate the tree's ultimate size, shade and beauty. Anyone leaving a legacy for his or her heirs knows that this loving gift will benefit those heirs and perhaps even benefit generations yet to come.

A friend of mine I knew during my high school years inherited so much money and assets when his dad died unexpectedly that he never had to work a day in his life. Of course, I'm certain he would have chosen his father more than the huge fortune he inherited.

The inheritance was his dad's loving provision for him from beyond the grave. Proverbs 13:22a (NKJV) tells us that "a good man leaves an inheritance to his children's children." This is one way we can easily see love reaching beyond the grave.

Christ died an earthly death; nevertheless, He did not simply forget His disciples. Since Christ knew He would suffer death and would leave this earthly plane, He gave His disciples authority over evil spirits and "opened their minds" (Luke 24:45a NIV). He also sent them "what My Father has promised" (Luke 24:49a NIV; see also Mark 6:7).

Jesus knew that in the world there was evil, disease and all manner of affliction. He was leaving His disciples a legacy of authority to exercise according to the will of God. Of course, He loved them and cared for them. He had personally selected each one of them, trusting them to continue on after He left.

Whenever we contemplate leaving or bequeathing something, it is not uncommon to also contemplate how the bequest will be used, enjoyed or maintained. As a lawyer, I have often seen bequests of parcels of land for some public benefit, such as a parcel of land being given to a municipality or county so long as it is used for a park.

Obviously, anyone giving such a gift with such conditions was no doubt a public-spirited person wanting to benefit others from beyond his or her lifetime. For something like a park or other public facility, the benefits would be enjoyed for generations to come.

Of course, the benefactor would have to trust that his or her wishes would be honored.

Jesus trusted that His disciples would continue His ministry, His work and His service to the people. So, when He "opened their minds" in Luke 24:45, He gave them a gift like no other—one that, in all things, they could continue as He began with the power of the gift. His love was pure, would endure all things, and would endure forever (see 1 Chron. 16:34).

In all of nature, mother animals protect their young against any foe. Even a perceived threat to the young will be met with extreme aggression. As for humans, I have often heard people say that one cannot know the love for a child until one becomes a parent.

Then, there is the love for a friend. Jesus taught us that there is no greater love than the love that causes one to lay down his (or her) life for his friends (see John 15:13). During World War II, Audie Murphy3 demonstrated that love when he climbed atop a burning tank and used its machine gun to prevent enemy advancement, allowing his fellow soldiers to retreat.

He was willing to give his life for his comrades-in-arms by deliberately placing himself in harm's way. After he single-handedly prevented enemy advancement and had rejoined his troops, he then led a counterattack. His selfless, singular efforts that day saved lives and prevented enemy advancement.

Audie Murphy received the Medal of Honor for his "indomitable" courage. It's apparent that he was willing to lay down his life and fight to the death if necessary. Although his actions demonstrate what the scripture references, please consider a love even greater: Christ's love for us!

In Christ's perfect love, He laid down His life for the world. No one could take or make Him give His life, since there was and is no power greater. He lay down His life willingly, and He did so for us.

Now, in thinking back on my own children's coming home after being born, I can remember the weeks of preparations: furnishing their nursery and stocking diapers and supplies to make everything ready. Of course, having never had children before, I was hopeful that I'd "gotten it together" so they would have everything they needed.

When Jesus departed after His resurrection, He told the disciples that He was going, that He would prepare a place for them, and that He would return to take them to the place He prepared so they could be with Him (see John 14:3). Christ had us in mind, not only from the beginning, but throughout time.

He came to redeem us from sin, remained among us during the time of His ministry on this earth, then returned to the Father to prepare a place for us to join Him later. And, unlike our human possibilities to forget something, overlook something or leave something incomplete, Jesus did not and will not.

God gave us His WORD in love!

## CHAPTER SIXTEEN

# Hope Encourages

Hope can be described as a desire combined with expectation. When we hope for something, we are desiring a favorable outcome or perhaps wanting something other than an unfavorable outcome. We cannot always predict a future that is certain, although we may very well offer an educated speculation, which, if it is based upon reliable information, could be extremely accurate.

Depending on our past experiences, our knowledge and available indicators, we may be able to predict with a degree of accuracy a good many things, such as weather, arrival time upon returning from a trip, how someone will react to certain news, or even whether someone will enjoy a gift we have selected for him or her.

However, we also may experience those times when we fear the worst while still hoping for the best. Someone awaiting lab results following a medical concern knows this feeling all too well. We have often heard of a situation being referred to as "hopeless." Some might use the word *impossible* to describe a situation where all hope is lost and the inevitable worst-case scenario is guaranteed.

I would say with near absolute certainty that almost everyone has faced a hopeless, desperate, impossible situation sometime during his or her lifetime. For many, this time of crisis may be the first time one turns to prayer. Perhaps later is better than never, though.

### Go to God First

Jesus said, "What is impossible with man is possible with God" (Luke 18:27 NIV). When we can't seem to do something on our own, we finally ask God to do it. There is no reason we can't and shouldn't ask God for His blessing and help first, instead of waiting until the last moment. Many times, when we finally get around to asking God to "step in," we have already made things worse and now want Him to "bail us out" of whatever predicament or out-of-control situation we have gotten ourselves into.

On the way down is not the time to remember we forgot our parachute. I'm sure God must feel frustrated watching how we managed to get ourselves into some of the situations we find ourselves in from time to time.

When Jesus was on the hillside near Galilee, ministering and healing people, several days elapsed. But before He left and before sending the people home, He knew they needed to be fed. The disciples informed Him that they had seven loaves and a few small fish.

There were 4,000 men, plus women and children. Before anything else, though, Jesus thanked God. Then everyone was fed, and there were seven baskets of food left. (See Matthew 15:29–38; Mark 8:1–9.) The example Jesus continually set shows us to first go to God, then proceed in accordance with His will.

The point is, before we totally ruin a situation or completely botch something beyond all possibility of remedy, we should first seek God. After all, our hope is in God, who teaches us and guides us in truth (see Ps. 25:5).

We are incapable of perfection or of total accuracy, and we are subject to error. "Human error" is an absolute. Anything of mankind is subject to the possibility of failure, error and inaccuracy. There is no possibility of error, mistake or inaccuracy with God, however. Regardless of our actions or the circumstances we may encounter, God has the answer. In doing our best, no one hopes for the worst. Our expectation is commensurate with the effort we expend in connection with a certain desire. So, naturally, we hope for the best, and what is better than God?

### God Is the Best

In business or other undertakings involving a partnership or combined effort such as a team effort or a group assignment, we hope that all of us working together are similarly motivated, interested and able. Perhaps we even hope some in the group are even more able.

If we have children playing organized sports, we might hope their team wins a big game or makes it to the playoffs. If we are working on a lab assignment at school, we might hope to impress the teacher and receive a good grade.

We might be involved in a contest to see which team can sell the most product. Regardless of the event or other specifics, when all things are equal and if everyone involved gives their best efforts and stays on task, then success is a reasonable expectation.

I remember, in high school chemistry lab, the teacher assigned a lesser able student to be my "lab partner." In those days we worked with Bunsen burners and actual hands-on chemical mixtures. I was discouraged with my lab partner because I felt that the chances of my receiving a good grade were unlikely.

I also knew that my partner wasn't capable of contributing much to the assignment. My only "hope" was that he wouldn't do something when my back was turned that might sabotage everything. Although I was cautiously proceeding, trying not to let him touch anything flammable, dangerous or critical, as soon as my back was turned for a brief moment, an explosion occurred, which totally ruined the experiment.

My partner had moved the flame of the Bunsen burner under a chemical mixture, causing it to explode and send glass shards, liquid chemical and debris all over our lab station and the immediate surroundings. No one was injured, fortunately, but I was not happy that the entire experiment was destroyed because of his carelessness!

Imagine how God must feel when we tackle something while depending on our own ability or effort, then totally ruin things. There is no reason for us to tempt failure when it so easy to partner with God through prayer. In His will, there is no failure, when we proceed accordingly.

When the disciples were feeding the multitudes, there was no shortage of food. Jesus had asked God's blessings first rather than after having already run out of food. Jesus didn't want anyone hungry, thanked God for the bread and fish at hand, then anticipated a favorable result. Just as Jesus had expected, all were fed with plenty left over.

Asking God ahead of time for His blessings is not to doubt one's own ability or motivation; it is quite the opposite. By putting prayer first, we are demonstrating a commitment by investing all we can give. Why would we ask God to bless some half-hearted investment or effort?

I truly don't believe He would be pleased knowing we expected Him to give His best when we weren't giving our best. Only in our best efforts in His will, with His blessings, do we have hope. If we are going to put it all on the line, then we certainly wouldn't want to guarantee failure.

In prayer, we are letting God know we trust Him for the right outcome. We aren't exhibiting self-doubt but exhibiting total confidence. When David selected five smooth stones from the stream, he wasn't doubting his ability with the sling; rather, he had total confidence in God.

He knew God only needed one stone, but he was going into battle overly prepared, intending to use his every ability to defeat Goliath and face anyone else whom he might have to face. David was not going to sling one rock and run! (See 1 Samuel 17:40–50.)

"Sustain me, my God, according to your promise, and I will live; do not let my hopes be dashed" (Ps. 119:116 NIV). If He gave His WORD, then He gave all. He gave His best, and there is no doubt He will continue to do so.

## CHAPTER SEVENTEEN

# Patience Is Required

I have heard the old saying that patience is a virtue. Indeed, there are times when patience is one of the more demanding of virtues. Anyone who has raised children knows the frustration of waiting. Children have their own timetable.

No child is alike, and no child learns the same skills in the exact same amount of time. Talking, walking, reading and innumerable other skills learned in childhood are things that we, as parents, cannot hurry. Our children, on the other hand, must wait also.

Everyone remembers waiting impatiently for Christmas to finally arrive, or for school to finally be out for the summer. Some children wait on their parents to finally "get things together." Unfortunately, some children wait in vain, hoping their parents will finally become the responsible, loving parents they have always needed.

### Be Patient

I know we all have also heard the phrase, "hurry up and wait," from the military. This phrase explains in one sentence how frustration feels.

When things take longer than we expect or than necessary, we feel this frustration and grow impatient.

We have also observed how trying to hurry usually results in mistakes. When we get in a hurry, we may forget a detail that we would not have forgotten had we stayed calm and focused and taken the necessary time. We may find ourselves rushing when we are running late for an appointment or for work or to get the children from school.

We may get lucky and arrive at our destination without being involved in an accident. We may arrive at work without the boss noticing we arrived a bit late. On the other hand, there are times we may realize that had we just taken a bit more time, or exhibited a bit more patience, we would have been better off.

Having to wait on someone or something beyond our control is a source of stress. Anyone who has dealt with a delayed or cancelled flight knows this stress. Time rules our lives to an extent, and it seems we are servants to the clock.

Busy parents have their calendars filled with practice times, doctor appointments, school functions, sleepovers, birthday parties, field trips and other activities. Having multiple children result in an exponential number of calendar entries.

Another judge who has been a friend of mine for some years has ten children ranging in ages from infant to teenager. Imagine his and his wife's schedules! I don't know how they manage, but I do know for a fact that they consider themselves blessed.

There is none among us who have not had to be patient at one time or another. In today's society, it seems that instant gratification has become the norm. Few practice patience. We can order food with a smart phone, pay with an app on our smart watch, and even deposit checks into our bank account instantly.

It is no wonder that some get impatient over even minor delays. It seems that society is becoming conditioned not to wait. Today's ease of travel allows us to be virtually anywhere in the world within a matter of hours rather than months. Any number of people who reside in colder areas of the country often have another home in a warmer region, such as Florida. These people avoid having to wait for the snow to melt to enjoy warmer weather; they can simply leave and travel to a warmer climate.

The Bible gives us any number of examples of individuals or groups waiting on God's timing. Proverbs 19:11 tells us that a man's wisdom gives him patience. Psalm 27:14b (NIV) admonishes us to wait for the Lord, to "be strong and take heart."

The Bible also tells us that love is patient and kind (see 1 Cor. 13:4). God's being love then also includes God's being patient and kind. Indeed, patience is a form of kindness. Being patient with someone could be the kindest, most loving thing others can do for that person.

For a moment, think back to a time when perhaps you weren't as patient as you could have been with someone; then think how that person must have felt afterward. I'm sure the person did not feel kindness or love. Perhaps he or she felt unimportant, unworthy, not valued or even not wanted.

If we are not inclined to patiently wait upon the Lord, would we want Him to feel that we did not want Him in our lives? Would we want Him to feel that we did not think He was important or His will was irrelevant?

Imagine how Jesus felt when He was praying in the Garden of Gethsemane and the disciples fell asleep twice while they were supposed to be patiently keeping watch (see Mark 14:37–41). I believe it is more difficult to be patient when we don't know how long we must wait.

Jesus apparently didn't tell the disciples how long to keep watch, and perhaps they became bored waiting. Notice how impatient children become during a car trip: the question, "Are we there yet?" will be heard more than once. I'm sure the disciples wondered how long they were expected to stay there keeping watch.

### Worth the Wait

After sending word to Jesus about Lazarus' being sick, I'm certain Mary and Martha wondered why Jesus was taking so long to return. We know that Jesus stayed away an additional two days after learning of Lazarus' situation (see John 11:6). When Jesus arrived, Lazarus had been dead a total of four days (see John 11:17).

Those four days must have seemed an eternity for Mary and Martha while waiting on Jesus. We can see in these passages that the sisters were sorrowful, and even Jesus wept. However, as anyone of that era knew, a dead body would be in a state of decomposition after four days.

Most certainly Jesus knew what everyone was thinking, and no one would doubt His divine being once Lazarus was raised from the dead after four days in the tomb (see John 11:43–44). We know from this miracle that patience is sometimes painful and not easy. But we also see that God's timing is always perfect in any given circumstance to accomplish His purposes.

Had Lazarus died with Jesus right there and been returned to life within an hour, there are probably those who might have claimed Lazarus was never really dead and all Jesus did was wake him from sleep. Remaining away an additional two days before going to raise Lazarus from the dead demonstrates Jesus' purpose in making Martha and Mary wait patiently.

I know that God wants us all to learn and practice more patience. I was raised by impatient parents who had little time or interest in me. I could never do anything fast enough or good enough to please them. I tend to be impatient with myself as a result.

Often it still feels like I am not going fast enough or finishing quickly enough. In writing, I see the finished book in my mind and want it to be done. However, it takes patience to write, and the chapters don't go from my thoughts onto the page instantly. It is a very thoughtful, technical, methodical and sometimes laborious, painstaking process.

I carry paper and pen with me so I can make notes as my mind constantly forms the information I want to relate. Every time I begin running a marathon, I realize just how far twenty-six and two-tenths miles is and that it will take over five hours of continuous running to reach the finish line. I've often remarked that God is trying to teach me more patience and using marathon running to do so!

Accomplishments take time, patience and perseverance. As I contemplate reaching a goal, finishing a project or meeting a deadline, I must often remind myself that God did not create everything in just one day.

I tend to be very goal-oriented and am always trying to be productive. Delays, whether my fault or not, frustrate me. I see what needs to be done, how it needs to be done, and when it should be finished. We are human, though. So it is with God's blessings, our best efforts and faithful patience that we will see God's perfect plan accomplished.

Jesus told His disciples, "In a little while you will see me no more, and then after a little while you will see me" (John 16:16 NIV). Not only did they wonder what He meant, but they also wondered how much time a "little while" was (see John 16:18).

Like on a car trip with children, when we tell them we'll be there in a "little while," they want to know how long is a "little while." God created all in six days and rested on the seventh. We would have trouble putting a small garden together in six days, but that was just a little while to God.

I remind myself often that passage of time is different with God. He was, is and will ever be. Eternity is infinite, but our human lifespan is measured in years that are finite on this earth. We count the passage of time according to our human perspective, so what we perceive as taking "too long" is only proceeding according to God's perfect timing.

Jesus must have used the phrase "a little while" so His disciples would know to wait without expecting "instantly." Think about the generations that passed from Adam, to Noah, to Moses, before God gave us His WORD with the birth of Jesus.

## CHAPTER EIGHTEEN

# The WORD Before

In our first chapter we discussed the opening passages of the Gospel of John: "In the beginning was the Word, and the Word was with God, and the Word was God. He was with God in the beginning" (1:1–2 NIV). "The Son is the radiance of God's glory and the exact representation of his being, sustaining all things by his powerful word" (Heb. 1:3a NIV).

### He Is Christ the Lord

The Gospel of Luke described in detail when Jesus was born and the circumstances of His birth. Joseph and Mary traveled to Bethlehem for the census, and, after arrival in Bethlehem, Mary gave birth to Jesus (see Luke 2:1–7).

Luke continues on, telling us how an angel appeared to shepherds on a hillside attending their flocks during the night and God's glory shown around them, frightening them (see Luke 2:8–9). The angel told the shepherds that Jesus, Christ the Lord, was born and how to find Him (see Luke 2:11–12). "Suddenly," after this proclamation, a great number of additional angels appeared, "praising God" (Luke 2:13 NIV).

For a moment, dwell upon this scene as described: Here were shepherds, just ordinary, working men, watching over their sheep after dark on a quiet hillside when, out of nowhere, appeared an angel of the Lord in such glory that it shown all around them.

The word *glory* likely doesn't completely describe how truly magnificent it looked, and the "glory," or great splendor, must have been of such a tremendous glow that the entire hillside was alight, allowing all the shepherds to observe this appearance.

Once the proclamation was made, then the scene became even more spectacular because a great number of additional angels appeared praising God. Those shepherds most certainly saw something more awesome than anything they had ever seen. Short of being in God's presence, I cannot imagine anything more awesome than a host of angels suddenly appearing in such magnificence that the night sky would be completely illuminated!

Those same shepherds were accustomed to watching over their herds at night, being on hillsides with the moon and stars shining overhead. As anyone who has ever been out camping at night away from city lights can attest, those stars above appear much clearer, brighter and more beautiful because theirs is the only light besides the moon that can be seen.

City lights often prevent us from seeing what we can see when we are far enough away from the interference of civilization. So, when those shepherds beheld angels appearing in "glory," they were, of course, frightened because this is something they were not accustomed to seeing. It was something they had never experienced, and it was far more magnificent than stars twinkling in the night sky.

The splendor of the angels likely flooded the entire hillsides for as far as eye could see. Few events would be more majestic than a host of angels appearing. *Awesome* is the only word that comes close to describing this unprecedented moment in time.

Other descriptions in the Bible also use the word *awesome* in relating God's unparalleled splendor, telling us that God comes in "awesome majesty," for example (Job 37:22b NIV). It was not that this singular event was the only thing that was awesome, however. In John 1:14 (NKJV), we are told that "the Word became flesh and dwelt among us....." This was the promise that was in place from before time (see Tit. 1:2).

Grace was given us in Jesus Christ before the beginning of time (see 2 Tim. 1:9). Jesus was chosen before the creation of the world (see 1 Pet. 1:20). Isaiah 40:5a (NIV) foretells the coming of the "glory of the Lord," so when the angels appeared to those shepherds, indeed this passage was fulfilled.

Jesus had glory with God before the world began (see John 17:5). We have perhaps not fully explored just how awesome the coming of the WORD was. But, in contemplating the angels' appearance announcing the fulfillment of the prophets, it was quite positively the most magnificent, spectacular, extraordinary and miraculous event ever.

Certainly, for those shepherds, who most certainly had never seen even one angel before, this sight of a multitude of angels was awesome, as was the announcement they brought. To say that those shepherds felt an overwhelming fear, reverence, admiration and joy all simultaneously would be an understatement. Likely nothing in our language could adequately express all they felt.

Truly there are some emotions we feel and understand that defy explanation in terms of verbal expression. Most likely those shepherds were uneducated, perhaps not even able to read or write, but they knew and understood what they witnessed and what they felt.

In thinking how they felt, let's not forget how those angels must have felt. They were proclaiming the most joyous thing they would ever get to announce—Christ the Lord was born (see Luke 2:11). Their singular honor and total joy could never be expressed adequately.

### He Is the Word

There are those who still refuse to believe, despite Jesus' telling us of His divinity throughout the passages in the New Testament. Jesus tells us that He and the Father "are one" (John 17:11b NIV). Further, He informs us in Luke 10:18 (NIV), "I saw Satan fall like lightning from heaven." And perhaps the most telling scripture of Christ in the entire Bible appears in John 10:30 (NIV), which states clearly, without equivocation, that "[Jesus] and the Father are one."

Jesus could not have witnessed Satan fall unless He already existed! Further passages tell us that He is "the way and the truth and the life" (John 14:6a NIV). Jesus told Philip that anyone who has seen Him (Jesus) has seen the Father (see John 14:9). John 1:2 (NIV) says, "He was with God in the beginning." Hebrews says, "The Son is the radiance of God's glory and the exact representation of his being, sustaining all things by his powerful word," through whom He made the universe (Heb. 1:3a NIV).

Jesus Christ is in "very nature God" (Phil. 2:6a NIV). We know these passages are fact because Jesus is incapable of lying or of any form of dishonesty. As mentioned in an earlier chapter, God never lies, His promises are never broken, and His guarantee was Jesus. God's word is truth (see John 17:17). "Dominion and awe belong to God" (Job 25:2a NIV).

The hope of eternal life was the guarantee. Hebrews 6:12b (NIV) tells us to be patient to "inherit what has been promised." This scripture does not say what *will be* promised or what *is being* promised or what *might* occur; it says what "*has been* promised." This is past tense, and it shows that, long before the beginning of time, God made this promise (see Tit. 1:2).

Remember that say we mentioned earlier, that "a man's word is his bond"? When we give our word on something, we are making a promise and giving a guarantee. In past times, a man's word was sufficient to convey what now, in modern time, must be written in the form of a contract, a court order, a deed, an affidavit or a sworn, written document. Human failings result in forgetfulness, reconsiderations and outright fraud.

Of course, we have the Bible, but remember, when God created everything, "in the beginning was the Word, and the Word was with God, and the Word was God" (John 1:1 NIV). There was no Bible then; there was no written language then; and God's Ten Commandments had not yet been carved on the tablets of stone. Instead, we had God's WORD! His promise was Jesus!

The Word, then, was not a written or spoken word, but *the* WORD, which was God's promise from before the beginning of time. The WORD was His guarantee of eternal life so that we could be with Him.

Jesus was that promise, that covenant, described as the WORD! God gave us His WORD, a promise that could not be broken, that He would redeem us to give us everlasting life through Jesus Christ.

Jesus became flesh, the living WORD, the promise of salvation. Words live on, long after being spoken or written. Thus it is in every way an appropriate term to refer to Jesus as the WORD because, just as words live on and cannot be unspoken once uttered, Christ lives on forever!

### The Plan

God had a purpose in creating earth, and He revealed to Isaiah how Christ would come (see Isa. 7:14). Christ's becoming flesh was the fulfillment of God's plan from before the beginning. So, God was relating His ultimate plan for us.

Jesus was the representation of God, and after Jesus came and "provided purification for sins, he sat down at the right hand of the Majesty in heaven" (Heb. 1:3b NIV). As Jesus once prayed, "Father, I want those you have given me to be with me where I am, and to see my glory, the glory you have given me because you loved me before the creation of the world" (John 17:24 NIV).

Clearly, God had a plan before the beginning that would not only bring all into being, but also would be sufficient to sustain all things, that would atone for sin, and that would give us a way to live on with Jesus. Obviously, God works everything out for His own ends (see Prov. 16:4).

Nothing is left to chance, accident, coincidence or afterthought. God simply did not create all things, then somewhere along the way decide maybe He'd better figure out something else. It is clear that the divine plan of the WORD preexisted.

William Marcy, a New York senator in the 1820s, made this saying famous in a speech: "To the victor belong the spoils."1 "Spoils" refer to the prize, reward, assets, benefits or treasure. Christ emerged triumphant over Satan's temptations and then death on the cross, and now He sits in heaven as the victor—to Him be glory and honor forever! To Him we belong, and we can choose eternal life.

Jesus said, "No one comes to the Father except through me" (John 14:6b NIV). The choice is ours because God gave us, as humans, free will. We can either receive the truth and believe it, or we can refuse to believe it.

Throughout the New Testament, Jesus taught using parables. Often, when He used a word or phrase, the actual spoken words were used allegorically. There was a deeper meaning behind the parable itself, also. "…Anyone who will not receive the kingdom of God like a little child will never enter it" (Luke 18:17 NIV).

Jesus was not saying that only children can enter Heaven and be with Him. Anyone who has raised children know how fully dependent, trusting and innocently confident they are in their parents. It is clear that Jesus was alluding to that level of faith and belief in Him as a requisite to eternal life.

We began the first chapter relating the scripture, "In the beginning was the Word, and the Word was with God, and the Word was God" (John 1:1 NIV). The "Word" did not refer to vocabulary; rather, the "Word" referred to the covenant, the promise, the guarantee being Jesus—the WORD! "In the hope of eternal life, which God, who does not lie, promised before the beginning of time" (Tit. 1:2 NIV).

Even though we don't know when, we do know the WORD will come again, as promised. And, again, it will be awesome! Indeed, I believe His second coming will be even more awesome, spectacular and inspiring than His birth. I believe this because it is then we will experience a new life without end.

## CHAPTER NINETEEN

# Final Thoughts and Commentary

When my children were very young, I used every opportunity possible for teaching moments. Usually, those instances involved my showing them rather than only telling them. I once caught a horned toad so I could show them that despite its fierce appearance, it could be held in the palm of their hands without harm.

Jesus voluntarily took human form, embraced suffering without complaint or flight, suffered death and then resurrected Himself. He *showed* everyone, including the disciples, His power over death. By resurrecting Himself, He proved His power over death and demonstrated He can also resurrect us.

He wanted to experience what His creation experienced, to feel mortality and to show us that there was more to life than just what we as mortals experience on this earth. Jesus told His disciples that salvation was possible with God, and then He *showed* them.

Imparting information verbally is not the same as demonstrating it. By showing us His power over death, He gave us a much deeper understanding of His oneness with the Father. He faced death without fear or hesitation, showing us we need not fear death.

## Jesus Paid the Price

"But God demonstrates his own love for us in this: While we were still sinners, Christ died for us" (Rom. 5:8 NIV). Sin entered the world through Adam and thereby brought death to all mankind. "...Death reigned from the time of Adam to the time of Moses..." (Rom. 5:14 NIV). Christ's death freed us from the wages of sin. "The death he died, he died to sin once for all; but the life he lives, he lives to God" (Rom. 6:10 NIV). Jesus took human form to become our sin offering (see Rom. 8:3).

There are times in everyone's life when the unbelievable, incredible, untenable or seemingly impossible situation arises. We may have doubts, not only about what to believe, but also about our own discernment. Others may doubt us or our abilities, and we may doubt ourselves because of what others say about us or what we may tell ourselves.

Our human knowledge, wisdom and discernment are lacking. A hasty decision invites regret. Any decision born from panic, fear, ignorance or indifference will nearly always not be the best decision. Not only may others pay a price for such a decision, but we will be the ones primarily paying for it.

More often than not, the "price" is one of consequences, which is usually a problem greater than initially presented. In retrospect, one may ask, "How could I have been so stupid?" Sin is costly, and we humans have no way of avoiding or overcoming death. Christ died for us, overcame death and was resurrected "...in order that we might bear fruit to God" (Rom. 7:4 NIV).

## Outside of Time

We all have a beginning and an end in this lifetime. It is clear from scripture that Christ has always been and remains ever so. He has seen everything from before time; He knows what we will face, understands us and still cares. What many will ask is, just where was Christ at the beginning of creation?

Christ was there from the beginning, then dwelled among us, was crucified, resurrected, returned to His heavenly realm, and there remains until He comes again. He saw all and knows all. He has known us from our beginning.

After reading this book, I trust that the information shared in it answers this question. The next question one may ask is, why did Christ come to us through a human birth? Christ could have just appeared at any given time to begin His earthly ministry without experiencing a birth, a childhood or a human existence. But such would not have fulfilled scripture. We must never lose sight of the fact that God does not lie or deceive.

The scripture, being inspired by God as His Word, is not misleading or inaccurate. God's purpose in foretelling the birth of Christ was to reveal His plan for our salvation. The Book of Isaiah tells us that it is only through Christ that we may enter heaven and be with God. "I am the way and the truth and the life. No one comes to the Father except through me" (John 14:6 NIV).

Everyone who believes in Jesus is saved from death and the wages of sin (see Rom. 10:9,13). Sin cannot redeem sin, but grace can redeem from sin, and that is what Jesus did for us. Being without sin allowed His self-sacrifice for the sin of all mankind to be the only way for mankind to enter Heaven.

Jesus, being without sin, was in Heaven from before the beginning, became flesh to dwell among us, and died an earthly death for us. Heaven cannot be corrupted by sinful beings. Jesus could return there, as He was without sin (see 1 John 3:6; 1 Pet. 2:22).

When the disciples asked Jesus how then sinful man could be saved, Jesus responded by telling them, "With man this is impossible, but with God all things are possible" (Matt. 19:25–26 NIV). So they were given this knowledge, but I believe they could not have fully understood it at that time.

He *showed* us so we can fully understand rather than only be informed. No corruption, evil, impurity or sin can exist in the holy realm. For this reason, Satan and the angels following him were cast out (see Isa. 14:12). Since those angels were forbidden from dwelling in the holy place, sinful humans would not have been allowed there, either.

This book is about a discernment of the "mysteries" of what we know about God and about understanding Jesus as never before. We can understand God is real because He came to us, from a real place, then returned to that place (we call it Heaven).

We can understand more fully the depth of His love. He demonstrated that love by experiencing what we feel, by experiencing our perception of everything human, including our desires, concerns, frustrations, fears and ultimately death itself. Godly ways are not human ways, but in human form He experienced our ways.

Though we no longer have access to the Tree of Life for immortality, we now have access to eternal life through the WORD. Jesus' last words on the cross were "it is finished" (John 19:30a NIV). He was not saying, "I am finished," but pronouncing completion of God's plan for our salvation and redemption.

The WORD existed from before time; the WORD created; the WORD came to dwell among us; the WORD overcame death; and the WORD then returned to whence He came to prepare a place for us eternally with Him.

May God, namely Christ, the WORD, in whom are all treasures of wisdom and knowledge abide, be glorified, exalted, praised and honored. *Glory to God! Glory to His WORD!*

My humble prayer is that this book
will impact your life
according to God's will
and that you will be blessed
with a greater understanding of Jesus.

# Endnotes

**Chapter Two**
1. Robert Schuller, Brainy Quotes, accessed August 30, 2024, https://www.brainyquote.com/quotes/robert_h_schuller_121372.

**Chapter Three**
1. Theodore Roosevelt, Brainy Quotes, accessed August 30, 2024, https://www.brainyquote.com/quotes/theodore_roosevelt_140484.

**Chapter Four**
1. Alexander Graham Bell, Brainy Quotes, accessed August 30, 2024, https://www.brainyquote.com/quotes/alexander_graham_bell_387728.

2. Benjamin Franklin, Brainy Quotes, accessed August 30, 2024, https://www.brainyquote.com/quotes/benjamin_franklin_138217.

**Chapter Six**
1. Vince Lombardi, Brainy Quotes, accessed August 30, 2024, https://www.brainyquote.com/quotes/vince_lombardi_122285.

**Chapter Eight**
1. This saying was first used in the Oregon Supreme Court case of *State v. Rader* in 1912. "Unring the Bell," The Idioms, accessed September 3, 2024, https://www.theidioms.com/unring-the-bell/.

2. The phrase was first used by humorist Richard Armour in the February 17, 1949, issue of *The Van Nuys News*. Alexander Atkins, "What Is the Origin of 'Hindsight is 20/20'?" blog, Atkins Bookshelf, 12/30/2020, https://atkinsbookshelf.wordpress.com/2020/12/30/what-is-the-origin-of-hindsight-is-20-20/.

**Chapter Ten**
1. Sarah Keating, "The violent attack that turned a man into a math genius," BBC, 8 July 2020, accessed August 26, 2024, https://www.bbc.com/future/article/20190411-the-violent-attack-that-turned-a-man-into-a-maths-genius.

2. Bruce Lee, Quotable Quote, Goodreads, accessed September 3, 2024, https://www.goodreads.com/quotes/4146-do-not-pray-for-an-easy-life-pray-for-the.

3. Bruce Lee, Quotable Quote, Goodreads, accessed September 3, 2024, https://www.goodreads.com/quotes/1116397-defeat-is-a-state-of-mind-no-one-is-ever.

**Chapter Thirteen**
1. George Eliot, Quotable Quote, Goodreads, accessed September 3, 2024, https://www.goodreads.com/quotes/444526-don-t-judge-a-book-by-its-cover.

**Chapter Fifteen**
1. Abraham Maslow, "A Theory of Human Motivation," *Psychological Review*, 1943, **50** (4): 370-396.

2. "Language deprivation experiments," Wikipedia, accessed September 4, 2024, https://en.wikipedia.org/wiki/Language_deprivation_experiments#:~:-text=An%20experiment%20allegedly%20carried%20out,demonstrate%20once%20their%20voices%20matured.

3. "Audie Murphy," Wikipedia, accessed September 4, 2024, https://en.wikipedia.org/wiki/Audie_Murphy.

**Chapter Eighteen**
1. "William L. Marcy," *Encyclopedia Britannica*, accessed October 1, 2024, https://www.britannica.com/biography/William-L-Marcy.